DUAL VISION
The Simona and Jerome Chazen Collection

DUAL VISION

THE SIMONA AND JEROME CHAZEN COLLECTION

with essays by David Revere McFadden,

Russell Panczenko, Ursula Ilse-Neuman,

and Jennifer Scanlan

Museum of Arts & Design
New York
2005

CREDITS

Museum of Arts & Design
40 West Fifty-third Street
New York, New York 10019
www.madmuseum.org

Dual Vision: The Simona and Jerome Chazen Collection is the catalogue for an exhibition of the same name organized by the Museum of Arts & Design. The exhibition is on view at MAD from May 26 through September 11, 2005, and at the Elvehjem Museum, Madison, Wisconsin, from October 7 through December 31, 2005.

The exhibition and publication were coordinated by Assistant Curator Jennifer Scanlan.

Published in the United States of America by the Museum of Arts & Design.
Printed in the United States of America on Parilux, acid-free paper, and typeset in Whitney, a font designed by Hoefler & Frere-Jones.

Library of Congress Control Number:
2005925054

ISBN: 1-890385-10-7

BOOK DESIGN
HvAD
Henk van Assen and Amanda Bowers

EDITOR
Nancy Preu

PRINTING
Meridian Printing, East Greenwich, Rhode Island

Jacket (top): Gerhard Richter, *Abstract Painting No. 623,* 1987, oil on canvas, © Gerhard Richter
Jacket (bottom): Jay Musler, *Cityscape Bowl,* 1989, blown and sandblasted glass, oil pigments

Photo credits: David Behl, all photographs except 61, 62, 93, 95 and jacket (top) Courtesy of Christies; 110 by D. James Dee; 172 and jacket (bottom) by Eva Heyd; 116 by Ric Murray; 167 by Joshua Nefsky; 138 by Doug Schaible; 80 by Rob Vinnedge; 165 by Janusz Walentynowicz

CONTENTS

6 FOREWORD

Holly Hotchner

Director, Museum of Arts & Design

10 **DUAL VISION**

A CONVERSATION WITH SIMONA AND JEROME CHAZEN

David Revere McFadden

Chief Curator and Vice President for Programs and Collections,

Museum of Arts & Design

20 **WINDOWS INTO THE SOUL:**

VISION AND THE PRESENCE OF SELF

David Revere McFadden

30 **DISCERNING TASTE: THE PAINTINGS**

Russell Panczenko

Director, Elvehjem Museum of Art, University of Wisconsin-Madison

42 **CONTEMPORARY AND TIMELESS:**

PERSPECTIVES ON HEADS IN THE CHAZEN COLLECTION

Ursula Ilse-Neuman

Curator, Museum of Arts & Design

52 **ILLUMINATING VISION:**

LIGHT IN ABSTRACT GLASS SCULPTURE

Jennifer Scanlan

Assistant Curator, Museum of Arts & Design

60 **CATALOGUE OF THE EXHIBITION**

176 ARTISTS' BIOGRAPHIES

198 INDEX

On the occasion of the Museum's fiftieth birthday it is appropriate to celebrate two individuals who have shaped the institution's past and will shape its future. Simona and Jerome Chazen, through their enlightened vision and now through their gift of important ceramic and glass works of art, will put their imprint on the Museum of Arts & Design for generations to come. It is their shared desire to create a new Museum that will properly honor the field of craft, arts, and design in the heart of New York City, where they have enjoyed so much of their lives.

The Chazens have been a vital part of the Museum for nearly three decades, and over this time they have made an extraordinary commitment to our institution. Jerry Chazen served as the chairman of our board of governors for many years, and Simona Chazen became a board member six years ago, taking a keen interest in helping to form our collections by becoming chairman of our Collections Committee. The Chazens' deep love of the arts, their connoisseurship of paintings, drawings, sculpture, craft and decorative arts, and their wholehearted pursuit of these many art forms have informed their dual vision.

The Chazens' remarkable collection is being shared with the public for the first time through *Dual Vision.* This exhibition and publication also celebrate the Chazens' generous decision to give many important masterpieces in their collection to the Museum of Arts & Design. Included in this permanent legacy are works by Robert Arneson, Dale Chihuly, Dominick Labino, Stanislav Libenský, William Morris, Mary Shaffer, and Lino Tagliapietra, among others.

The Chazens' introduction to the Museum and the field of craft was in the 1980s, through the Museum's newly formed educational and travel group the Collectors Circle. Each year the Collectors Circle organized study trips to cities around the United States and abroad. These trips gave participants the opportunity to meet collectors with similar interests, view private collections, and meet artists from around the world. Through these early encounters, the Chazens nurtured deep friendships with artists, many of whose works are now in their collection, as well as with some of America's greatest collectors. In fact, it should be noted that the less tangible but equally precious part of the Chazens' collection is the circle of artist friends and collectors with whom they share their interests.

The Chazens have been courageous pioneers in their commitment to new talent and new art forms. From the outset they acquired works by artists who went on to become legendary, such as Harvey Littleton and Dale Chihuly, leaders of what was then the emerging field of studio glass. Over the years these relationships grew, and they came to know not only the first generation of studio glass artists but two subsequent generations, as well.

While the Chazens' collecting goals were expansive, they have always considered their glass and ceramics to be as significant as their paintings, drawings, and sculpture. When acquiring major works in glass, they also focused on paintings by American modern masters such as Robert Motherwell, Larry Rivers, and Richard Lindner. Sculpture by Jim Dine sits comfortably in their home beside glass and ceramic pieces by Stanislav Libenský, Erwin Eisch, and Sergei Isupov.

With the move to our new museum at Two Columbus Circle, the Chazen gift will become the cornerstone of a world-class collection, and the art the Chazens have so lovingly cared for will delight and inspire a new generation of collectors, students, and young artists. I wish to express our profound admiration and gratitude to Simona and Jerry for sharing with us their dream for the new Museum of Arts & Design, their vision as collectors, and their belief in the significance of art in all of our lives.

Holly Hotchner, Director
Museum of Arts & Design

David Revere McFadden

DUAL VISION: A CONVERSATION WITH SIMONA AND JEROME CHAZEN

These comments are taken from a conversation between the Chazens and David Revere McFadden, Chief Curator, Museum of Arts & Design, about the history of the Chazens' collection and their personal philosophies on collecting. This conversation took place in the Chazens' New York apartment in the summer of 2004.

SIMONA   I have always been a collector. I grew up in a Victorian home, and my parents collected nineteenth- and early-twentieth-century furniture, silver, bronzes, porcelains, glass, prints, and paintings to furnish it. They scouted second-hand shops for many of these things, and my mother once came home with a treasure nobody else wanted. It was a Tiffany floriform vase in perfect condition—and it cost five dollars. So, the idea of living with beautiful and interesting things was natural to me. My mother was also a sculptor in wood and clay. She studied with Chaim Gross and Seymour Lipton. Although I still have a collection of antique napkin rings that I use, as I matured my interests focused on modern art.

JERRY   My collecting interests began when I was young, but my passions were baseball cards and jazz records. This was back in the days when early 78 rpm discs could be found at second-hand stores. I have given up baseball cards, but my love of jazz will never end. My interest in the visual arts came later. Then, when circumstances allowed me to collect important contemporary art, I discovered glass. Our first purchases were from a craft gallery that featured glass by Orient and Flume and vases by Donald Carlson. Very shortly afterward, we purchased a large globe by Robert Palusky. I was hooked.

SIMONA   We were always interested in art but couldn't afford original paintings, so we started with lithographs and wood cuts. Some of those early prints by Hockney, Rivers, Rosenquist, Lichtenstein, and others still hang on our walls.

JERRY   I never had a grand plan for building a collection when I started out. Fortunately I was exposed to glass made by some of the leading figures in the American studio glass movement, such as Harvey Littleton and Dale Chihuly, and I realized that we could own important works of art and be supportive of living artists.

SIMONA   Luckily, Jerry and I then came into contact with some of the very earliest galleries that showed contemporary glass, the three H's: Holsten, Heller, and Habatat. This was back in the early eighties, and I remember the exciting day we purchased two Harvey Littletons and a Mark Peiser, our first really important acquisitions at Holsten. Having lived in Detroit for a period in our lives, we visited there frequently and found Habatat. We also met Dale Chihuly early on and bought several beautiful works, including a great one at a CGCA [Creative Glass Center of America] auction held at the Heller Gallery in New York. We believe Chihuly, in addition to being a wonderful artist, is also the greatest voice for art glass of the twentieth century, and perhaps the twenty-first.

JERRY   What is it that so appeals to me about glass? I have always found color to be seductive. I think this feeling comes through in our paintings and ceramics as well. But, as a medium, glass alone has that magical quality of color that is brought to life with light.

SIMONA   We also seek content and emotion in our collecting. A work of art in any medium has to appeal to both of us viscerally and visually, whether figurative or abstract.

JERRY   When we began as nascent collectors, a new group, the Collectors Circle, had been formed at the American Craft Museum, which, of course, today is the Museum of Arts & Design. Because of my involvement with the Collectors Circle, I eventually became chairman of the Museum and held the position for many years. Simona is co-chairman of the Collections Committee. The Collectors Circle opened up a whole new world. We shared our interests with other collectors and visited them when we traveled. The world of craft artists and collectors was much smaller then, and people were unbelievably generous about opening their homes and studios to us. We learned a lot.

SIMONA   Do we always agree on what we choose for the collection? Not always, but certainly a lot of the time. Our individual points of view, as well as our shared vision, shape the character of the collection. We do have one rule that vetoes a purchase: if the other person absolutely hates it, we don't buy it.

JERRY   Another source of learning and inspiration for us was an early trip to the Corning Museum of Glass, where we saw Italian and Scandinavian glass and the memorable work of Stanislav Libenský and Jaraslova Brychtová. Through them, we discovered the kind of sculptural glass that was related to our interest in modern art.

SIMONA   And we should not forget the importance of the *New Glass* exhibition and publication of the Corning Museum of Glass, which highlighted one hundred upcoming artists each year. Few books on contemporary glass were available, and most artists were entirely new to us. These exhibitions were seminal.

JERRY   An added benefit of our decision to collect glass was that the artists who were making this work were alive and approachable, and we have developed friendships with many of them. In fact, most of the founders and artistic leaders of the studio glass movement are still alive today, which is unusual for most fields of art.

SIMONA   A trip to the Scandinavian countries expanded our vistas considerably. For example, in Sweden we discovered Bertil Vallien's work. When he came to the U.S., he was a guest in our apartment and slept in a Murphy bed that came out of the wall, which intrigued him because he had never seen one before.

JERRY   Simona and I love the objects we live with every day. They give us pleasure every time we see them. I would suppose that the best way to describe our collection is "focused eclecticism." We believe that paintings and sculpture and craft are born from the same creative spirit and are happiest when they live with one another.

SIMONA   How did we discover other works in the collection, such as our paintings? We both had a few courses in art appreciation in college and knew we liked modern art. We visited museums and galleries, and for me the auction house was a school of visual literacy as well as a place to buy art. I made a point of visiting frequently when there were upcoming sales related to our interests.

JERRY   This was not blind collecting. We looked very carefully at the artist's track record and the significance to the field in general. If we had an initial positive visceral reaction to a painting, we then gave careful consideration to owning it. Was it something that would be treasured in the future as it is today? Is this an artist who has helped to shape the profile of the field?

SIMONA   And then came the real challenge—where to put it? Space is always a problem, but the question of the art works living easily with one another is not. We discovered that we usually choose bold colors in a similar palette and that, without really realizing it, a guiding aesthetic governs our choices. The visual dialogues that we see between our paintings, glass, ceramics, and sculpture are deeply gratifying.

JERRY   Simona and I had an informal "wish" list of artists and art works we wanted to acquire, and we kept after them until we could find what we really wanted. To choose one example, it took us ten years of looking to find just the right Gerhard Richter. We found "our" Motherwell and "our" Stella after a lot of looking, too. Our collection is not intended to include every major artist but the best work of the artist's best period.

SIMONA   We do collect a few artists in greater depth. As a lover of cubist sculpture, I am thrilled to have works by Archipenko and Lipchitz. In the glass collection, one of our favored artists is Mary Shaffer, whose work with slumped glass captures the energy and movement of the material in a particularly poetic manner. We feel the same way about Bill Morris's pieces and have quite a few works by him, as well as by Dale Chihuly.

JERRY   Milton Avery, Richard Pousette-Dart, and Jean Dubuffet are among the painters who are represented in some depth in our collection. Both of us want our collection to be a personal panorama that expresses who we are.

SIMONA   I am always asked, "What is your favorite work of art?" My answer is, "I don't know if I can answer that because I love all my children." We have never sold anything and have discarded very little of what we have bought in the last twenty-five years.

JERRY   Among my favorites is *Another Pretty Face* by Ginny Ruffner, a work that brings many aspects of our world together. The work has a beautifully painted surface that echoes our love of painting, and the subject matter is the history of art. The figures are drawn from iconic historical paintings by such artists as Picasso and Ingres. We've never set up any artificial lines between the various categories of art. Howard Ben Tré's powerful glass *Second Flask* lives easily with Jacques Lipchitz's cubist bronze *Tête* and Mel Kendrick's abstract sculpture.

SIMONA   To respond to the question of whether or not we admire virtuoso craftsmanship, I believe that virtuoso workmanship should always be in the service of meaning. In the realm of paintings, John Wilde is a truly superb draftsman; his complex and subtle paintings, drawings, and silver points give the subjects of these works an eerie and haunting reality. The artist exposes his inner self through his works. Unlike other contemporary artists, he does not express himself in abstraction but in painstaking documentation of the real and surreal people and objects in the landscapes of his imagination.

JERRY We have also collected the porcelain works of Sergei Isupov, who, through his detailed drawings and strange convoluted figures, also offers the viewer an intense and surreal visual experience. I would agree that we do not collect virtuoso works just because of the artist's technical skill. Take the work of William Morris. He is at the top of the league of glassblowers, but what makes him great is that his work is imbued with a poetry and sense of history that is expressed through his excellent craftsmanship.

SIMONA In looking over the collections, it is interesting to note that we are not usually collectors of vessels. While we can appreciate the value of these objects in our daily lives, we are drawn to strong figural work or powerful abstractions and little in between. While many of our paintings are studies in geometry, such as the Lichtensteins or the Burgoyne Diller, another body of work is organic and textural, such as the Pousette-Darts.

JERRY In the end, we have to have art around us that we want to look at and to live with.

SIMONA How would I define beauty? For me something beautiful is a delight to the eye, and that includes grotesque beauty as well. I have always thought the human body was very beautiful and that might help to explain our lifelong interest in works that celebrate the body. This is not only true for our paintings but also for our sculpture.

JERRY For me beauty is not necessarily beautiful in the sense of pretty or attractive. Something "beautiful" engages your eye and imagination, triggers an emotional response, or calls up a memory. When I stop to think about it, it is probably the same reason I find such satisfaction in music. It engages my full attention.

SIMONA If I were to advise beginning collectors, I would undoubtedly tell them that they are on a potentially thrilling quest of discovery. Any collector should look, look, look. This is why museums, auction houses, and galleries are such a great resource. This is how you develop your own taste and come to rely upon it. You learn to trust your eye, to know which works of art are derivative and which break new ground. You learn which are merely facile and which have true quality and lasting meaning.

JERRY I would have to agree with Simona that a collector must have a ravenous visual appetite and look at all the exhibitions and collections he or she can. While the Internet may be a useful place to find images, you never get to know the work of art until you have seen it in person. Any collection should convey the spirit of the collectors. I would also add that you should be very open to new artists, new art forms, and new ideas. If you enjoy meeting artists, this is a wonderful way to learn about how the artist sees. But you still have to respond to art in your own personal way.

SIMONA   What is the future of our collection? Our children will have some of it, but we hope that many of our treasures will be enjoyed by future generations who come to the Museum of Arts & Design.

JERRY   We have works by more than two hundred artists in glass, ceramic, and other media. They were all carefully chosen for their artistic excellence, and I wish we could mention every artist by name. Ultimately we are only stewards of these objects. The art will go on after us. In the meantime, collecting it has been a labor of love for Simona and me.

Jerome and Simona Chazen in their New York apartment, May 2003

David Revere McFadden

WINDOWS INTO THE SOUL: VISION AND THE PRESENCE OF SELF

1

Donald Elkins, *The Object Stares Back: On the Nature of Seeing* (New York: Harcourt Brace & Company, 1996).

2

Ibid., 237.

3

Philipp Blom, *To Have and To Hold: An Intimate History of Collectors and Collecting* (New York: Overlook Press, 2002), 191.

4

Werner Muensterberger, *Collecting, An Unruly Passion: Psychological Perspectives* (New York: Harcourt Brace and Company, 1994), 10.

In his intriguing and often unsettling book *The Object Stares Back,*[1] art historian Donald Elkins proposes that vision, like our own sense of self, is never static, nor are the images that inhabit our visual landscapes permanent and fixed: ". . . vision is forever incomplete and uncontrollable because it is used to shape our sense of what we are. Objects molt and alter in accord with what we need them to be, and we change ourselves by the mere act of seeing."[2] There is an ironic contradiction in defining what it means to collect: on one hand, the collector is assembling and preserving a body of works for posterity, yet the objects so gathered continue to evolve in their meanings over the lifetime of the collector and beyond. It might be suggested that collecting is a variant form of writing one's autobiography. "Every collection is a theatre of memories, a dramatization and a mise-en-scène of personal and collective pasts, of a remembered childhood and of remembrance after death. It guarantees these memories through the objects evoking them."[3]

It is not difficult to understand that any collection is ultimately about the foci of interests—aesthetic, social, economic, technical, or political—that energize the collector, and, at the same time, also about the collector's intimate and private reflections on beauty, meaning and, ultimately, the self. Werner Muensterberger's controversial but perceptive commentary on the context and goal of collecting is apt: "Some people remember a favorite toy; others recall the first attempts at collecting baseball cards or campaign buttons, or perhaps going in search of shells or minerals. [A collection] guarantees the presence of these memories through the objects evoking them. It is more even than a symbolic presence. . . . Still, despite all possible variations there is reason to believe that the true source of the habit is the emotional state leading to a more or less perpetual attempt to surround oneself with magically potent objects."[4]

The extraordinary collection assembled by Simona and Jerome Chazen over the past four decades is an eloquent record of the life passion of two individuals, each with his or her own vision and definition of art, but it is also that of a partnership in which these two visions are united in a coherent and significant way. To appreciate the Chazen collection fully, it is essential to see their objects—paintings, drawings, and sculpture in glass, clay, and metal—as a seamless and continuous spectrum of the arts. Painting lives comfortably with other mediums, and, in the Chazens' own residences, each work is thoughtfully and carefully placed so that it interacts with neighboring objects and the overall architectural environment. Works are distributed between the Chazens' gracious Frank Lloyd Wright–inspired home on the Hudson River and their aerie with 360-degree views of the city from the top of a Manhattan apartment building. Both settings, rural and urban, have been filled with objects that express their vision.

The Chazen collection includes art from around the world, primarily by artists who are still living and working today. There are objects of tremendous elegance and refinement, such as Steven Weinberg's *Cast Crystal Cube* [P. 78], Lino Tagliapietra's graceful blown-glass *Red Dinosaur #705* [P. 69], and Tom Patti's hypnotic sculpture of laminated glass, *Solarized Blue* [P. 98]. Other works are compelling for their spiritual and psychological presence, such as Flora Mace and Joey Kirkpatrick's *Vision with Likeness* [P. 94], one of their most memorable works in blown glass, comprised of two ghost-like figures eternally linked to each other. Powerful and large-scale sculpture includes Stanislav Libenský and Jaroslava Brychtová's *The Column* [P. 166], an imposing angular totem of glowing cast glass. The collection also has many other aspects that give it its own special character, some whimsical, such as Judy McKie's *Panthers* coffee table in bronze and glass [P. 156] and Dan Dailey's *Chandelier* [P. 137], depicting a bacchanal of stylized nudes, a work commissioned by the Chazens for their Manhattan residence. Some are provocatively humorous; Donald Lipski's *Pilchuck #90–21,* made of sheet glass slumped into a recycled French fry basket comes to mind [P. 63], as does Janusz Walentynowicz's unforgettable *Yellow Twelve Pack* [P. 165], a dozen rolls of glass toilet paper that glow as if lit from within.

What is it that gives the Chazen collection its unity? What links works in such diverse mediums to each other and to the collectors' visions? There are many themes that weave the Chazen collection into a seamless tapestry of visual, emotional, and intellectual explorations; some of these are revealed in the conversation with the Chazens in this volume. Others appear more clearly when the collection is presented as a mixed media ensemble. The Chazen collection invites us to create links and bridges among the works and, in so doing, to express our own vision of art, but it also asks us to join the collectors on the personal journey of looking, discussing, comparing, and contrasting.

Several underlying themes might serve as doorways or guideposts leading into the collectors' eyes and minds. These themes embrace and welcome the diversity of the artists' own visions, gently and quietly knitting them together with the collectors' thoughts and visions.

The themes include the depiction of different states of being, both physical and psychological, as revealed through the human figure; metamorphosis and change over time as a metaphor for life and as a means of perceiving "time" in a work of art; and lastly, a selection of the works examine time, but from the vantage point of history, written as fact or fiction.

IN THE BODY AND OUT OF THE BODY

Simona Chazen is a clinical social worker. Jerome Chazen is a business entrepreneur whose success has depended on his awareness of subtle changes in public taste. It is not surprising that a substantial number of works collected by the couple address perennial changes in states of being, both physical and psychological.

The work of the recently deceased sculptor Viola Frey is represented in the Chazen collection by two pieces, including an imposing (over seven-foot-high) figure, *Reflective Woman II* [P. 146]. Frey was one of the pioneers in the renaissance of interest in clay as a sculptural medium that occurred in California in the 1950s. Her monumental and garishly painted figures have become a hallmark of her oeuvre. They were produced by hand-building a complete figure and slicing it into sections that were painted and glazed. The pieces were reassembled to create the complete figure. Frey's *Reflective Woman* stands expectantly, as though waiting for someone familiar. At the same time, the almost authoritative posture and face suggest hesitation and even alienation. Frey captured these intense emotions in outsized figures that self-consciously refer to eighteenth-century traditions of delicately painted porcelain figurines and their nineteenth- and twentieth-century kitsch descendants—knickknacks. This creates a powerful tension between the evocations of historical standards of value and beauty and our modern appreciation of the confrontational potential of art.

British sculptor Sir Anthony Caro is well known for his abstract and geometric constructions in metal, but he also produces more organic and figural works, particularly in clay, intentionally disregarding artificial hierarchies and barriers that have been used to separate ceramics from the larger field of sculpture in general. Caro's *Mister* [P. 104] belongs to a series of works that explore the timeless presence of the figure. The standing male figure is shown as a fragment of the body, lopped off at the knees and neck. The references to classical Greek male nudes are clear; Caro has long been inspired by ancient history, myths, and literature. At the same time, a strong sense of person emanates from the fragment. We do not have any face and minimal references to specific body parts to help us understand who the figure might represent (it is, indeed, an anonymous "mister"); however, the posture and body language are eloquent in their evocation of this strong, confident, and determined individual. The emotional and spiritual content of the figure is evoked with grandeur even in these fragments.

Rudy Autio refers to the tradition of vessel making in his work but exploits the outer surface of the pot by using it as a canvas upon which he paints overlapping figural studies. The Chazen collection contains his 1988 *Day and Night* [P. 154], a work that admirably represents his style and approach to figuration. The figures that encircle the vessel are choreographed to carefully overlap or contrast with each other; the artist bridges the work of craft, painting, and sculpture by giving the core vessel a highly sculptural and animated profile on which limbs or other body elements are transformed into three-dimensional shapes.

If Autio expresses the exuberance of the human figure in motion, a darker side permeates the work of Russian-born Sergei Isupov. Like Autio, Isupov challenges our expectations about both his chosen material—porcelain—and sculptural form. Art historian Glen Brown writes that Isupov's distinctive take on the human figure continues into his selection of format: "Their absolute identity as paintings, sculptures or ceramics cannot be determined."[5] Isupov's *To Keep in Touch* [P. 149] is filled with a physical and emotional tension portrayed in the writhing and contorted forms; the result can be read by the viewer as either a dream or a nightmare, or a curious amalgamation of both. While Isupov's work is dynamically three-dimensional, the Calibanesque character of his figures is reiterated in the accomplished drawing on the porcelain surfaces. His background as a printmaker becomes apparent in these fine-lined images in which every intimate detail of a body or face is recorded. The intensity of Isupov's faces is echoed in another haunting work in the Chazen collection: a painting by American artist John Wilde entitled *Work Reconsidered #2. A Portrait of Jesper Dribble* [P. 148]. This is a spellbinding and unsettling glimpse of the artist analyzing himself in a canvas mirror. We are drawn to the figure, but at the same time the oval frame reminds us that we can never truly enter the artist's private world.

Ann Wolff's *Spider Woman* [P. 131] comes from a body of work produced in the 1980s that deals with highly abstract evocations of the human figure, and whose titles primarily suggest ancient goddesses or figures of ritual significance. Wolff is a prime example of the seamlessness among mediums that can be seen at virtually every turn in the Chazen collection. She began as an artist in glass, moved into painting and drawing, and ultimately merged her sculptural and painterly interests in figures such as this. German art historian and critic Verena Tafel has noted that, in these works, Ann Wolff focused her artistic vision on ". . . the gestural language of the entire body. The mirrored image of the inner state became the major theme."[6]

Like Viola Frey, Manuel Neri was a member of the highly influential group of artists that emerged in the San Francisco Bay area around the mid–twentieth century. Neri immediately began questioning the rules about materials used to make art and their relative artistic and cultural values, choosing to work in "junk" such as burlap and plaster. His sculptures are

5
Glen Brown, "Sergei Isupov: On Multi-Stable Ground," *Ceramics Art and Perception,* no. 51 (March 2003), 41.

6
Essay in the exhibition catalogue for *Ann Wolff,* a retrospective touring exhibition organized by Heller Gallery, New York, March 7 through March 28, 1987, publisher unknown.

highly expressionistic, conveying a sense of the purity of classical Greek and Roman figures, while his rough, highly textured surfaces recall modern expressionist paintings. Like Jim Dine (whose large painted bronze sculpture *Venusberg* is also found in the Chazen collection [P. 152]), Neri turned his back on the beautiful luster and patina of bronze by painting the figures, thus obscuring the prized foundation material. Neri's female figures are generally inspired by his model, as is the eponymous *Remaking of Mary Julia No. 2* [P. 67]. In many ways this figure conveys the same isolation and anonymity of a classical sculpture removed from its original context. Neri poses the question of whether or not the figure suggests loneliness or self-realization, a theme that the sculptor has investigated throughout his career.

THE TIME OF CHANGE

The process of change and evolution is inevitable in our lives, but also in inanimate objects. Through works of art, we are able to "see" time as well as timelessness, which may be a factor influencing the sense of engagement, contemplation, and pleasure that emanates from a collection, whether displayed in private or public. Thoughtful collectors also realize that the works they have judiciously assembled are revelatory of another kind of time—that which the artist has invested in creating the object, and that embedded in the process of collecting. "Time," wrote the Argentinean author Jorge Luis Borges, "is the substance of which I am made. Time is a river that carries me along, but I am the river; it is a tiger that devours me, but I am the tiger; it is a fire that consumes me, but I am the fire."[7] Time carries meaning only when we realize that we are time itself.

The evolution of time in the world of non-human nature is captured in such sensuous organic forms as Dale Chihuly's blown-glass *Macchia Basket* [P. 159] and Marvin Lipofsky's lush undulating *Pilchuck Summer Series #4* [P. 153]. Chihuly's familiar forms are most often compared to supple and ever-changing underwater invertebrates. Actually they seem to hover somewhere between the water and the air, their rippling profiles seducing the viewer's eye through color and the transmission of light. The Italian word *macchia,* which roughly translated means a spot or stain, seems an appropriate description of the radiant, jewel-like splashes of color on the work, but the meaning of the term goes much deeper, to include the idea of the origins of the creative gesture itself, what Robert Hobbs has called ". . . the spontaneous outpouring of artistic sensibility."[8]

Other artists in the Chazen collection catch time in a stop-motion gesture, a unique moment in time, that is now preserved in tangible form. Glass is particularly adept at capturing this quality, and it is not surprising that many artists use this material to create visual metaphors of time and memory. Daniel Clayman's *Ripple* [P. 134] situates a vibrating demi-egg of translucent glass inside a bronze container, the shape suggesting a dried seed pod at the end of autumn—broken open, seeds dispersed, and now filled with the icy reminder of winter and

7
From "A New Refutation of Time," in *Labyrinths: Selected Stories & Other Writings,* ed. Donald A. Yates and James E. Irby (New York: New Directions Books, 1962), 234.

8
Robert Hobbs, "Reflections on Chihuly's Macchia," in the exhibition catalogue *Chihuly Alla Macchia from the George R. Stroemple Collection* (Beaumont, Texas: Art Museum of South Texas, 1993), [9–10].

the passing away of the corporeal. Mary Shaffer's *Hanging Series Water—White #3* [P. 141] connotes the fluid inconsistency of water in motion, but also the rippling effect of wind on a transparent cloth. Like Clayman, Shaffer brings the qualities of glass and metal into play in an unexpected way. Shaffer's work also carries a subliminal message about the finality and inescapability of change; in this work, Shaffer's glass passages are trapped in an intractable wire mesh. Shaffer's work is haunting and mysterious, transforming discarded metal fragments such as this piece of mesh, forgotten rusty tools (often used in other work by this artist), and humble slumped or cast transparent glass into emotion-charged touchstones for memory and fantasy.

Time and the process of decay and erosion have intrigued both American and European artists. *Laminated Glass Sculpture* by Hungarian artist Maria Lugossy [P. 99] is comprised of a pyramid of clear laminated glass, immediately bringing to mind the timeless permanence of an Egyptian pyramid. Lugossy's pyramid, however, acknowledges that change and decay are inevitable; the purity of the geometric planes of the pyramid has been eroded to create gaps in the structure. Lugossy's work admits the inevitability of natural forces; other works by this artist take on the appearance of landscapes or even entire planets caught in a precious moment of erosion that precedes total extinction.

American artist Michael Glancy also evokes the eroded surfaces of landscape in his richly textured compositions, such as *Cloaked Ruby Sentinel* [P. 161]. Glancy utilizes both a vessel form and a platform, the latter functioning much like a presentoir for this unique object. The surfaces of Glancy's vessels immediately bring to mind the time- and water-etched landscapes of the American Southwest viewed from the air, or even the mysterious eroded channels we have now seen on Mars. Glancy's eroded streams and tributaries are not empty, but filled with bronze that has been electrodeposited in the grooves, suggesting that the channels once flowed with another material that has been petrified over time. There is also a sense of repaired damage in his work, recalling the gold infill used to mend a prized cracked tea bowl in Japan.

TELLING TIME

A final group of objects in the Chazen collection approach time as tangible reality and also as historical narrative, fiction, or stories that we create in response to their forms. These works are ultimately about art and the history of art; each provides a glimpse into the emotional investment required to make history meaningful on a personal and cultural level.

American artist Ginny Ruffner offers the viewer her own editorial "take" on the history of art in her work *Another Pretty Face* [P. 88]. This flameworked and painted piece is a compendium of familiar images of women drawn from the history of Western art. Each woman is depicted as an icon of her time, a permanent record of how the concept of beauty has been constructed and deconstructed over the centuries. Appropriately for the female iconography, the lush organic vines and flowers that intertwine with the painted images suggest fecundity. They also become a dense jungle in which the truth of any given moment in women's history has been overlaid with political, sexual, and aesthetic baggage that nearly obscures the individual. As revealed in this work, Ruffner's commentary on feminism is both a celebration and an indictment of the entire history of art.

The Swedish sculptor Bertil Vallien is internationally known for his poetic and dreamlike cast glass compositions that often take the form of a generic boat, as is the case with *Boats and Bars* in the Chazen collection [P. 144]. The archetypal boat shape immediately brings to mind the carefully carved and painted miniature boats, replete with servants, food, and other supplies, that accompanied Egyptian nobility into their tombs in order that they enjoy life after death. Vallien's boats appear to have been sunken in water; the detritus that floats within the vessel's hull includes recognizable artifacts as well as mysterious fragments. Vallien's boat is a repository of memories precise as well as vague, a metaphor for history itself. We write the narrative that accompanies the boat, each viewer "reading" the contents and writing his or her own story.

The last example of time embedded in object and history, and one of the most dramatic, is William Morris's *Raft* [P. 80], a multi-part composition of animals, horns, and fragments of vessels. Archaeological associations are immediately suggested by Morris's forms; the objects are simulacra of a prehistoric and preliterate world from which only objects and fragments remain as witnesses to the past. Morris's artifacts are receptacles, containers, and preservers of memory, history, and culture. In this work they are also gathered as a collection, not a random assemblage. While the ritual implications of their shapes may be indecipherable to us, they do remind us that the making of art and the collecting of art are uniquely human traits. Clearly the world of collecting begins with our human origins.

In their collection, the Chazens have written a memorable autobiography through the objects with which they live. They have also contributed significantly to the larger story of why art is made, and why it is loved, preserved, and transmitted from one generation to another. The audience invited to read both histories—of collectors and a collection—has expanded geometrically with the Chazens' decision to make their collection a gift to the Museum of Arts & Design and to the world at large.

Russell Panczenko

DISCERNING TASTE: THE PAINTINGS

Private individuals differ from professional curators in that their collecting is not confined by museum policies. They do not have to be taxonomists, striving to exemplify and preserve for future generations the artistic developments and achievements of a particular time, place, or culture, nor do they have to be critics and adhere to a set of abstract principles. The relationship between the work of art and the private collector is direct and personal. Collectors can find beauty where they see it. This freedom is particularly enviable when it results in a truly outstanding collection such as that of Simona and Jerome Chazen. Within the broad range of their collecting interests, the Chazens' paintings are especially noteworthy. Theirs is a collection that includes some of the most beautiful work by some of the most important artists of the twentieth century. It is a collection of which any museum in the world would be proud.

The Chazens' primary criterion in collecting paintings has always been beauty or appeal to the "eye." Adhering to a time-tested form of connoisseurship, they return repeatedly to a gallery or an artist's studio, asking themselves if they like the painting in question as much the third and fourth times as they did the first. Only if the answer is a persistent yes do they finally make the acquisition. The Chazens do not go out of their way to pursue works by the most important artists; there are paintings in the collection by less well known artists whose works have equal pride of place on the walls in the Chazens' home.

The Chazens' collection of paintings ranges in time from Arshile Gorky's *Madonna and Child* of 1937 to John Wilde's *Myself in the Great War* of 1999. Most of the paintings are by American artists, although there are several works by Europeans, most notably Jean Dubuffet, David Hockney, and Gerhard Richter. Three artists, Richard Lindner, Jean-Paul Riopelle, and even Hans Hofmann, can be said to have had a foot on both the North American and European continents. Joaquín Torres-García and Jesús Rafael Soto are South Americans.

Although geography is one way of circumscribing the breadth of this collection, it has never been a motivating factor in the Chazens' decisions. A large percentage of the Chazens' paintings are nonfigurative and abstract. A subset within this group hints at a preference for modernist clarity in, and even a rational, impersonal approach to, composition. There are two fine examples of geometric abstraction from the second quarter of the twentieth century: the striking *Red Tondo* by Ilya Bolotowsky [P. 118], and an austere, untitled black-and-white painting by John McLaughlin [P. 95]. The very attractive *Untitled #285* of 1942 by Ed Garman [P. 93], with its pop colors and effervescent forms, is superficially related to these works but, in fact, represents the short-lived southwestern transcendentalist variety of content-driven American abstraction dependent on the style and philosophy of Wassily Kandinsky. Burgoyne Diller's *First Theme* of 1962 [P. 123], also a fine example of geometric abstraction, was painted after the ascendancy of abstract expressionism in the 1950s and Diller's rebirth, as far as contemporary critics were concerned, as a minimalist.

Three elegant abstract paintings by the also poet, novelist, and journalist Charles Green Shaw, one of which, *Abstraction with Blue, Brown, and Gray Forms,* is included in the current exhibition [P. 167], are forerunners of the more purely geometric style of the artists mentioned above. However, the compositions of Shaw's paintings were determined more by the artist's intuition about what looks right than by the dictates of geometry and the straightedge. His paintings also have another quality that makes them particularly attractive and clearly indicates the artist's mastery of the subtleties inherent in his medium: a precious, skin-like paint surface, that is smooth from a distance but rich and delicately textured to the eye that approaches for close observation.

Two later works in the Chazens' collection that basically display the same formal qualities as those of geometric abstraction are the large canvas entitled *Imperfect Painting* produced in 1988 by Roy Lichtenstein [PP. 150–1] and the 1985 mixed-media piece *Diagonal Virtue* by Jesús Rafael Soto [P. 100]. Obviously these artists are working from very different perspectives, one in New York, the other in Paris.

Lichtenstein always had an interest in geometric abstraction because of its "naïve quality of believing that logic would make art."[1] Already in 1964 he produced two works in the style of Mondrian. During the late sixties he produced works based on the geometry of art deco. Later, in the Imperfect paintings, done between 1986 and 1988, the rigid geometry of the composition, which is made up entirely of interlocking triangles, is only relieved by the decorative op effects of regularly applied dot patterns and/or parallel lines. In each of these paintings, the artist physically extended one or more corners of a triangle contained within the composition beyond the perfect rectangular frame. The composition of the Chazens' *Imperfect Painting* is even more complex. Not only do two triangles in the upper left physically extend beyond the confines of the rectangular canvas, but there is the implication of another large triangle, defined by the black and white pulsating line pattern, covered in part by other triangles, extending far beyond the confines of the canvas. Only a small part of this triangle is visible; the rest is left to the viewer's imagination.

1
Diane Waldman, *Roy Lichtenstein* (New York: Solomon R. Guggenheim Museum, 1993), 167–9, 271–7.

2

Ibid., 243.

3

See "Excerpts from an Interview with Soto," in *Soto: A Retrospective Exhibition* (New York: Solomon R. Guggenheim Museum, 1974), 8–21.

4

Ibid., 7.

5

For this fact and other information contained here, see Margit Rowell, "Order and Symbol: The European and American Sources of Torres-García's Constructivism," in *Torres-García: Grid-Pattern-Sign: Paris-Montevideo 1924–1944* (London: Arts Council of Great Britain, 1986), 9–20 [catalogue of an exhibition at Hayward Gallery, London, November 14, 1985–February 23, 1986].

A second painting by Roy Lichtenstein, entitled *Two Figures* [PP. 108-9], basically displays these same formal qualities. However, in addition, it tells a story: an anthropomorphic configuration of robust masculine triangles, standing in a desert and casting a shadow out of the picture plane, meets a curvaceous blue-eyed blonde, with prominent red lips. A distant pyramid tells us that this encounter takes place in Egypt. This painting is one of several surrealist works that Lichtenstein produced in the late 1970s. According to Diane Waldman, "what attracted him to Surrealism was its very orthodoxy; it contained within it, like comic strips or consumer-product ads . . . the seeds of a stereotype."[2]

Soto, who left Venezuela in 1950, was self-professedly inspired by the work of Mondrian, Malevich, Klee, and Albers.[3] However, he was not satisfied with the static metaphysics of geometric abstraction. For him, art also had to reflect the continually changing nature of the world. Thus early on Soto began to search for a way to represent movement, either mechanical or optical, in his work. Tom Messer, the former director of the Solomon R. Guggenheim Museum, put it succinctly: "Soto related Calder's physical to Vasarely's optical kineticism."[4] The Chazens' *Diagonal Virtue* is an excellent example of his three-dimensional moiré style.

Joaquín Torres-García, who in 1943 painted the Chazens' beautiful *Constructive a Cinco Colores con Locomotora Azul* [P. 65], was also influenced by geometric abstraction. After his early training in Barcelona, Torres-García spent the years 1920 to 1922 in New York experimenting with a schematic graphic style and then went to Paris where he fell under the influence of Piet Mondrian's neo-plasticism and particularly the ideal geometry of Theo van Doesburg. Based on this experience, he soon developed a style that he called "universal constructivism."[5] However, although his paintings always have an underlying rational structure, ultimately, his work is not about geometry. While in Paris, Torres-García also became an ardent admirer of pre-Columbian art as a key to the unconscious, an interest that continued and expanded throughout the rest of his life. The artist structured the surface of *Constructive a Cinco Colores con Locomotora Azul* into a grid, as he did with most of his paintings; however, in this painting he filled the sections of the grid not with anthropomorphic and mystical symbols, but with schematic visual references to the contemporary industrial and urban realities of Montevideo, the city where he was born and where he settled on his return to Uruguay in 1943. In addition to a modern ship (Montevideo is a port city), and the train mentioned in the title, the name of the city appears in one of the grid-sections.

This may be a good place to mention *Mirror Shadow xxxxv* by Louise Nevelson [P. 106]. Dated 1987, it, like the painting by Torres-García, consists of small compartments stacked one upon another, each of which contains some objects. However, the shapes within Nevelson's box-like structures are neither anthropomorphic nor symbolic, and the unity of the whole is not based on an intellectual or geometric idea. Rather, this wall relief was assembled intuitively, and, in order to give it unity, the artist painted the entire construction black.

In the mid and late 1950s, Hans Hofmann began to assemble his painterly compositions out of heavily color-laden rectangles.[6] Although the Chazens' untitled painting of 1950 by this important teacher and artist [P. 97] already exhibits some of this characteristic but somewhat later compositional device, it strongly reflects his European origins, particularly the influence of Matisse and, in this instance, synthetic cubism. As was often the case between the mid-1930s and late 1940s, Hofmann seems to have turned to a room interior for his initial inspiration for this ultimately very abstract composition. A yellow table with a pineapple on it and a picture hanging on the wall within the picture, which were common motifs in Hofmann's earlier interior scenes,[7] both appear here, one in the center of the composition, the other in the upper right, and both have become flat design elements far removed from their original models. The Chazens' painting by Hofmann also exhibits that quality that particularly endeared the artist's work to Clement Greenberg and made him particularly welcome among the ranks of the abstract expressionists, i.e., his "animated painterly surface."[8] His paint looks and acts like paint and is applied and pushed around on the surface of the canvas, now with a brush, now with a palette knife, and sometimes directly out of the tube.

A number of American artists in the mid–twentieth century adopted the biomorphism of Miró and the abstract surrealists. The best representation of this development in the Chazens' collection is *Forms: Transcendental* by Richard Pousette-Dart [P. 112], which was painted in 1950, a year before the artist's more or less permanent withdrawal from the intensity of the New York City art scene. Under the influence of the painter, theorist, and collector of tribal art John Graham,[9] Pousette-Dart, early in his career, developed a strong interest in primitivism and the role of the unconscious in the creative act. To this, as exemplified in *Forms: Transcendental,* he added a menagerie of mythic personages, animals, and symbols. Eyes abound throughout the composition and anthropomorphic figures emerge, first one, then another.

The other two paintings by Pousette-Dart in the Chazens' collection epitomize later stages of his richly creative career: *Grael of Light* [P. 135], which was painted in 1966–67, and *Myth of the Calyx* [P. 68] from 1979. *Grael of Light* (with the archaic spelling of *grail* that was used extensively by the Pre-Raphaelites) exemplifies a lesson Pousette-Dart learned from the granular structure of film, namely that "all form is made up of so many points of light and that everything has a miniscule molecular structure."[10] The artist, like the impressionist or pointillist painters of the late nineteenth century, patiently and painstakingly applied his

6
It is interesting to note that two other artists who structured their compositions either geometrically or with some kind of a grid system, and whose work is represented in the Chazens' collection, studied with Hans Hofmann: Burgoyne Diller and Louise Nevelson.

7
See Cynthia Goodman, *Hans Hofmann* (New York: Abbeville Press, 1986), 37.

8
For the definition of *painterly,* see Walter Darby Bannard, "Introduction," in *Hans Hofmann: A Retrospective Exhibition* (Houston: The Museum of Fine Arts, 1976), 11.

9
Sam Hunter, "Richard Pousette-Dart's Spiritual Quest," in *Transcending Abstraction: Richard Pousette-Dart, Paintings 1939–1985* (Fort Lauderdale, Fla.: Fort Lauderdale Museum of the Arts, 1986), 9–11.

10
Judith Higgins, "To the Point of Vision: A Profile of Richard Pousette-Dart," in *Transcending Abstraction, Richard Pousette-Dart, Paintings 1939–1985* (Fort Lauderdale, Fla.: Fort Lauderdale Museum of the Arts, 1986), 20.

pigments, point by point, and layer upon layer, until he achieved the overall wholeness of the bright light effect he desired. From a distance, the painting appears simple in composition; up close, one discovers a deep, rich, dense, multicolored surface that is its own miniature world. *Myth of the Calyx,* primarily black and white with a subtle touch of primary color here and there, is inhabited by numerous small squares, triangles, and other incomplete geometric forms.

Perhaps the most important example of abstract expressionist painting in the Chazens' collection is *Elegy to the Spanish Republic #125* by Robert Motherwell [PP. 126-7]. Between 1948 and 1990, beginning with a small ink drawing to illustrate a poem by Harold Rosenberg, the artist created a series of over two hundred paintings devoted to the theme of the Spanish Civil War. The Chazens' *Elegy,* whose design closely resembles a small painting of 1949 entitled *At Five in the Afternoon,*[11] was painted in 1972. Its composition, like that of most of the Elegies, consists of a metrical cadence of freely painted vertical forms compressing round ones. The composition is rendered primarily in stark black and white, Motherwell's main colors for over thirty years. In style the painting is gestural and appears completely nonobjective. However, the title clearly points to an important historical event, which, although it began in 1936 when the artist was only twenty-one years old, left him with a profound lifelong impression. Motherwell was unusual among the abstract expressionists in that he allowed references to historical, literary, and philosophical concerns in his work as long as they dealt with universals rather than specifics. There are various interpretations of the Spanish Elegies. When asked, Motherwell himself said of them: "Black is death, anxiety; white is life, *éclat.*"[12]

Toward the end of the 1950s, a number of artists grew restless with the rhetoric of action painting and its insistence on the elimination of consciousness from the creative process. As the renowned analyst of twentieth-century American art Irving Sandler has so aptly pointed out, chief among them was Al Held.[13] Held's successful search for a new personal alternative to abstract expressionism, which first manifests itself in 1959, resulted in a new body of work, his "concrete abstractions," of which the Chazens' untitled painting of 1960 [P. 120] is an outstanding example. In it the artist renders simplified forms, circles, squares, and xs and zigzags in bright primary colors. The subject is aggressively non-objective, devoid of any emotional content, but, at the same time, the paint is applied freehand and allowed to drip and run down the canvas; there is no geometric precision.

Formally and spiritually related to the painting by Al Held is Alexander Calder's strikingly graphic gouache on paper of 1965 called *Mountain Range* [PP. 76-77]. Calder painted with gouaches for most of his life, preferring this medium to both oil and watercolor because of the bright colors and ease of use. In his autobiography, Calder made many passing refer-

11
For an illustration of *At Five in the Afternoon,* see Dore Ashton, "On Motherwell," in *Robert Motherwell* (New York: Abbeville Press, 1983), 35 [catalogue of an exhibition at the Albright-Knox Gallery].

12
Ibid., 10.

13
Irving Sandler, *Al Held* (New York: Hudson Hills Press, 1984), 27.

14

Jean Lipman, *Calder's Universe* (New York: Viking Press, in cooperation with the Whitney Museum of American Art, 1976), 119–20.

15

William S. Rubin, *Frank Stella* (New York: Museum of Modern Art, 1970), 22.

16

Robert Storr, *Gerhard Richter: Forty Years of Painting* (New York: Museum of Modern Art, 2002), 15.

ences to scenery that impressed him[14] and, later, in a windowless studio, produced abstracted designs based on what he had seen.

Another extraordinarily fine painting, which echoes the reaction to the emotional content and form of abstract expressionism, but which unfortunately could not be included in the present exhibition because of its size, is *Double Scramble* by Frank Stella [PP. 102-3]. Executed in 1978, it is a later version of a compositional scheme that Stella first employed in the early sixties. Stella, a highly intellectual artist, had turned to simplified linear geometry for its impersonal character early in his career. In his concentric squares, first used in 1961, Stella, also found the "absolute bilateral symmetry" that he believed would not only give his paintings a holistic oneness but also eliminate all implications of illusionistic space that, for him, were still present in abstract geometric painting.[15] The most successful early concentric square paintings were rendered in varying values of gray. The early color versions, which used primary and secondary colors straight from the manufacturer Benjamin Moore, and whose arrangement was strictly determined by a designer's color wheel, were less satisfactory from a purely aesthetic point of view. In the later *Double Scramble,* the colors, although still primaries and secondaries, have been selected and arranged according to the artist's intuition. And, by this point, Stella's understanding and use of polychromy had been greatly refined and personalized, making *Double Scramble* not only intellectually highly satisfying but aesthetically as well.

One of the most visually striking paintings in the Chazens' collection is Gerhard Richter's *Abstract Painting No. 623* of 1987 [P. 61]. In this excellent example from an important body of work that the artist refers to as his "Abstract Pictures,"[16] bright, vibrant, sometimes even strident, colors are generously applied again and again, layer over layer, with a brush or a hard-edged instrument. No layer ever completely obliterates the layer below, and in the process, colors are sometimes mixed and muddied. Although he was never thought of as a colorist, Richter, in the Chazens' painting, as in others in this series, uses color to evoke highly energized, but nonetheless controlled, atmospheric effects that are the equal of those created more than a century earlier by William Turner. Reflecting for a moment on the Chazens' taste, this author cannot but note that here, as in the later two works by Pousette-Dart, the painting by Hans Hofmann, and, in a much more subtle way, those by Charles Shaw, discussed above, the visibility and tactile qualities of paint applied to canvas are significant contributors to the beauty and aesthetic effect. Other works in the collection that exhibit a similar painterly quality are those by Byron Browne, Jean-Paul Riopelle, and Alfred Jensen, as well as the Sandro Chia discussed below.

In 1973, the Guggenheim Museum presented a retrospective exhibition of the work of Jean Dubuffet, which later traveled to the Grand Palais in Paris. At both venues a theater-like

17

Jean Dubuffet 1943–1963, Paintings, Sculptures, Assemblages (Washington, D.C.: Hirshhorn Museum and Sculpture Garden, in association with the Smithsonian Institution Press, 1993), 144.

18

See Jean Dubuffet, "Coucou Bazar: Jean Dubuffet's Directions for Staging and Music," in *Jean Dubuffet: Towards an Alternative Reality* (New York: Pace, Abbeville Press, 1987), 237–40.

19

Andreas Franzke, *Dubuffet*, trans. Robert Erich Wolf (New York: Abrams, 1981), 227–28.

20

Richard Kalina, "David Hockney at André Emmerich," *Art in America* (May 1993): 117–18.

installation, named *Coucou Bazar, Bal du l'Hourloupe* (Cuckoo Bazaar, Ball of the Hourloupe) excited the imaginations of many. According to the artist "*l'hourloupe* is a word whose invention was based upon sound. In French these sounds suggest some wonderland or grotesque object or creature, while at the same time they evoke something rumbling and threatening with tragic overtones."[17] The images associated with the hourloupe cycle began for Dubuffet as subconscious ballpoint pen doodles; later they became paintings and relief sculptures, and finally architectural and theatrical environments. Some even became costumes for moving figures in the *Coucou Bazar.* The Chazens' wonderful *Danse Elance* [PP. 84-5], although created in 1971, appeared in both 1973 presentations of the *Coucou Bazar.* Dubuffet dubbed such pieces "*practicables,*" by which he meant that they were pieces of painted scenery that, at the same time, had independent existences as works of art.[18] This dynamic cutout assembly of shapes outlined in black on a white ground—some of which are filled with blue or red, others embellished with blue or red stripes—is the most irregular of the Chazens' "shaped canvases."

Dubuffet's *Inspection du Territoire* [P. 105] belongs to a series of paintings called Castilian landscapes, which were the last manifestations of the Hourloupe cycle.[19] Dubuffet made the original drawings for the paintings in this series with a felt-tip pen in the late spring and summer of 1974. Subsequently, his assistants enlarged them onto canvas. As in most of them, a figure stands in a light ochre and black landscape with a light blue sky overhead. Rendering the figure itself in red, blue, and black on white ground makes it stand forth from the landscape itself.

Although not explicitly theatrical in intent, David Hockney's *The Sixteenth V.N. Painting* of 1992 (V.N. stands for Very New) [P. 132] calls to mind the artist's stage sets, particularly his recent design for the opera *Turandot.* This character, which was already noted by Richard Kalina in the first published review of this work, makes it appropriate to juxtapose it here with Dubuffet's *Coucou Bazar.* There is something in their general intent to which the Chazens, themselves avid music lovers and theatergoers, may have reacted. As Kalina so aptly pointed out about this series of twenty-six paintings, "Looking at them we feel as if we are in the balcony of a darkened theater. . . . There is an air of expectation about them, a sense that something musical and extravagant is about to happen."[20] At the same time, this painting is rich in color, shapes, forms, and a variety of decorative effects. It is truly a painting to be enjoyed sensually.

The focus of this essay has been mainly on the abstract paintings. However, figurative work is also well represented in the Chazens' collection. Above, in the two paintings by Roy Lichtenstein, we have already seen an inclination toward pop art. Three other artists in the

21

Sam Hunter, *Larry Rivers* (New York: Rizzoli, 1989), 28–9.

22

Marco Livingstone, "Telling it like it is," in *Tom Wesselmann* (Tübingen: Cantz Verlag, 1996), 9 [catalogue for an exhibition organized by Institut für Kulturaustausch, Tübingen].

23

Richard Lindner, *Catalogue Raisonné of Paintings, Watercolours, and Drawings,* ed. Werner Spies, comp. Claudia Loyal (Munich: Prestel, 1999), nos. 2407–81. It is interesting to note that drawings nos. 479 and 480, which were done in 1953, already show the same basic composition as that of *L'as de trèfle,* although at that time the composition was intended for a work called *The Visitor.*

24

Eleanor Heartney, "Apocalyptic visions, Arcadian dreams," in *Art News* 85 (January 1986): 87–88.

25

In a personal statement the artist wrote: "[Works of art] se non sono gli occhi dello spirito e degli angeli, almeno siano i loro occhiali!" [if they are not the eyes of the spirit and of the angels should at least be their eyeglasses] in *Passione per L'arte, Sandro Chia, Leidenschaft für die Kunst* (Bielefeld: Karl Kerberg, 1986), 10.

26

See for example Franz Marc's *Horse in a Landscape,* of 1910, which is in the Museum Folkwang in Essen and illustrated in Christian von Holst, "The Hoofbeat of My Horses," in *Franz Marc: Horses* (Ostfildern-Ruit, Germany: Hatje Cantz, 2000), 77, pl. 60.

Chazens' collection can also be listed under this rubric: Larry Rivers, Tom Wesselmann, and, to a lesser degree, Richard Lindner.

The *Last Civil War Veteran* [P. 71], one of a famous series of paintings on this subject that Larry Rivers started in 1959 and continued into the seventies, is based on photographs that the artist saw in *Life* magazine.[21] Rivers, who is often classified as a pop artist because of his use of popular and commercial images, worked mostly in a loose, painterly way associated with the action painters. The Chazens' *Last Civil War Veteran* is not as loosely painted as some of the earlier versions. The narrative components of the scene, the flags, the bed and pillow, the uniform, and even the highly decorative floral pattern on the wallpaper at the top are clearly defined as in the original photograph. The artist's expressionistic intensity is effectively concentrated in the old general's arms lying pathetically on top of the blanket.

Tom Wesselmann's shaped and shapely *Stockinged Nude with Fishbowl* [PP. 90-1] is unabashedly what it is. A committed pop artist, Wesselmann, at the very beginning of his career, determined that he was not going to be an abstract painter.[22] He turned to the urban world around him for inspiration, transmuting commercialized cultural clichés into arresting works of art. Soft-core sexuality, which was being used increasingly to advertise products of all sorts, became one of his primary subjects. In fact, one might say that his beautifully sensual, but impersonal, depictions of pure sexuality sold his paintings as well.

A very remarkable and arresting figurative painting in the collection is Richard Lindner's *"L'as de trèfle"* (The Ace of Clubs) [P. 164]. Born in Germany in 1901, Lindner, fleeing the Nazis, went to Paris in 1933 and then to New York in 1941. He made his living as a commercial artist and illustrator of books and popular magazines (e.g., *Town and Country* and *Vogue*) in both Europe and America until the late 1950s. Because he became a painter late in life and only produced a very small number of finished works each year, his paintings are rare. Almost eighty preparatory drawings attest to the study and care that went into the creation of *L'as de trèfle,* which was completed in 1973.[23] Although painted in New York, the subject of this carefully controlled composition seems to hark back in spirit to the cabarets of Germany between the wars.

Artists of the so-called Italian *transavanguardia* "borrow freely from art of the past . . . and then transform [the images] through exuberant brushwork into mysterious personal visions."[24] *Horseman in Front of the Sea* by Sandro Chia [P. 81], which was painted in 1986, is an outstanding example of this search for the sublime.[25] In a scene that is both romantic and reminiscent of Franz Marc,[26] Chia's horseman, far removed from the cares of the everyday world, contemplates the sun setting into a hotly painted sea. The lush painterly surface has much in common with those of several paintings previously discussed above.

27

Information provided to the author by the artist in a telephone conversation on December 13, 2004.

28

Theodore F. Wolff, *Wildeworld, The Art of John Wilde* (New York: Hudson Hills Press, in association with the Elvehjem Museum of Art, University of Wisconsin-Madison, 1999), 17.

The last painting on which I will comment, knowing that it is one of Mrs. Chazen's favorites, is *Work Reconsidered #2. A Portrait of Jesper Dribble* by John Wilde [P. 148]. The painting is actually a self-portrait and is based on one of two silverpoint drawings by this artist, called "the wedding portraits," which are today in the collection of the Whitney Museum of American Art. Jesper Dibble is the name that appears on an old gravestone that Wilde found in an antique shop and uses today as a cocktail table in his home.[27] The inclusion of a name from a headstone is not surprising in the work of this Midwestern magic realist who often alludes to death in his work.[28] In addition to being an excellent likeness, this exquisitely painted memento mori includes the artist's age: "*AE [aetas] 38*," as well as the painting's date, on the small folded paper floating in front of him. It is one of many self-portraits Wilde has painted in the course of his life, in each stating his age either in the work itself or in the title.

There are numerous other paintings, both abstract and figurative, in this extensive and wonderful collection on which I have not commented, not for any lack of interest but because of a lack of time and space. Given these practical considerations, my intention has been to highlight what I believe to be some of the collectors' favorite paintings in hope of shedding some light on their taste and interests in this area. However, there are other fine paintings in the collection, some by such well known figures as Milton Avery, Arshile Gorky, and Philip Pearlstein, others by less well known artists such as Attilio Salemme and Ida Kohlmeyer, that would certainly add to our understanding.

In closing it might be interesting to make several general observations. All the paintings in the Chazens' collection are visually striking. There is a marked predilection for strong primary colors and graphic clarity. A majority of the paintings are nonrepresentational, and many of these can be characterized as nonobjective. Even those paintings where some form of figuration is present, except for the Pearlstein, are still largely abstract. All the paintings are extremely well executed; each artist is a master of his medium. In addition one might note an interest in irregularly shaped canvases, of which there are several examples in the collection.

Many of the artists represented in the Chazens' painting collection, in one sense or another, belonged to that school of modern art that sought to express spiritual, idealistic, or at least nonmaterial values in their work and ascribed to the general tenet of the age that a way to achieve this was to emulate the formal purity of music. A number of the Chazens' favorite painters were directly involved with music. For example, early in his life Roy Lichtenstein was passionate about jazz; his first subjects were jazz musicians. At age seventeen, Larry Grossberg changed his name to Larry Rivers and began a musical career as a jazz saxophonist. He later studied at the Julliard School of Music. His first encounter with art was through

29
Franzke, *Dubuffet*, 209–10.

a musical motif based on a painting by Braque. Dubuffet's *Coucou Bazar* was accompanied in 1973 by music composed by the Turkish composer Ilhan Mimaroglu. Later, for its 1978 reincarnation in Turin, Dubuffet composed the music himself.[29] Soto also was an accomplished guitarist of popular music, and various critics have seen the influence of music in his work. Musical sound is even an element of Soto's latest installations: they chime as one brushes against them. Pousette-Dart, although not a musician himself, was very interested in correspondences between music and the visual arts, an intellectual curiosity that he inherited from his mother, Flora, who was both a musician and a published poet. Gerhard Richter's mother, too, was a musician, and later he, like Pousette-Dart, was fascinated by the relationship between art and music. Is it coincidence then that the Chazens, who are also passionate music lovers, should show a preference for this kind of art? Or is it tacit recognition of kindred spirits?

Ursula Ilse-Neuman

CONTEMPORARY AND TIMELESS: PERSPECTIVES ON HEADS IN THE CHAZEN COLLECTION

Images of the human head are universally understood, communicating their messages from one age to another, across geographic and cultural boundaries. Throughout history, artists have presented the human face as a screen on which the inner self is projected—the eyes reveal thoughts and moods, the mouth underscores this message with a smile or a scream, a raised eyebrow or flared nostrils betray subtler emotional nuances. The collection of contemporary masterworks that Simona and Jerome Chazen have assembled is replete with works that renew and enlarge the expressive potential of this timeless symbol of the human condition.

Viewing the figurative works in the Chazen collection from a historical perspective reminds us that portrait heads reflect the concerns and values of the societies that create them. In Western art, an ongoing dialogue on the nature of the individual can be discerned through portraits in which subjects are presented as unique beings and those in which they are presented as impersonal embodiments of human ideals, whether philosophical, social, or aesthetic. In early Greek portraiture, for example, the figure typically conformed to a Platonic ideal, or a paradigm of physical beauty, while in the later Hellenic period, when the existence of Greek civilization was threatened, individuals were portrayed with idiosyncratic features and inner complexity. Over the centuries, Roman portraits also ranged between idealized images and presentations of the fuller personality.

Portrayals of character or personality were generally absent in medieval figures, but in the Renaissance, a revolutionary change in worldview initiated a new age of portraiture that combined antique models with the humanist's interest in the individual. Leonardo da Vinci exemplified this transformation in thinking by capturing subtleties in facial expression and pose that penetrated the external defenses of the sitter to reveal "the motions of the mind."

From the Renaissance to the nineteenth century, conventions dictated which expressions were appropriate in portraiture, with extremes of emotion generally avoided. In a dramatic about face, these conventions were attacked in the beginning of the twentieth century. The stark brutalities of World War I and the dehumanizing aspects of the industrial age both contributed to a breakdown of restraints on Western sensibilities and rendered obsolete the superficial decorum that typified earlier portraits. The rise of sociology as a discipline, indicating that mankind itself was a viable object of study, along with the arrival of Sigmund Freud's theories concerning the subconscious, compounded the change. In no time, artists began translating these new insights into portraits suffused with the erotic desires, neuroses, and previously taboo feelings that were thought to lie behind the visage.

A remarkable expansion in portraiture came at the hands of several significant sculptors of the modern era. In particular, the genre evolved as a result of Rodin's demonstration that a body fragment such as an arm could be a fully expressive work of art. In portraiture, this concept was reflected in a shift in focus from the traditional portrait bust to the head. Following Rodin's innovations, Brancusi pushed allegorical portraiture almost to the point of abstraction, so that a small oval with only the slightest marks to indicate a child's face could serve as a monument to innocence or human potential.

The pioneering work of Picasso and Braque also synthesized new ideas in radical ways. Picasso's strikingly asymmetric and psychologically perceptive 1906 *Portrait of Gertrude Stein,* for example, marks a significant moment in the history of the portrait head genre. Inspired by non-Western artifacts such as African masks, as well as by the latest revelations of psychoanalysis, Picasso discovered a way to make visible the complex matrix of desires and anxieties underlying the composed face that heretofore had been the subject matter of portraiture. Freed from the demands of mimesis, Picasso and his peers depicted individuals in more oblique ways than had been explored previously. Their challenging approaches to the study of the head revitalized the ancient genre of portraiture and ensured that it would be a subject to which contemporary artists would return again and again.

Jacques Lipchitz considered his 1915 *Tête* (Head), a mainstay of the Chazen collection [P. 62], to be the first sculpture successfully to translate the complex cubist idiom into three dimensions. Created when Lipchitz came under Picasso's sway, the piece unites concepts of subject and form, using architectural planes to suggest the features and proportions of the human head. Working in conventional bronze-sculpting techniques, Lipchitz used a variety of textures, patinated surfaces, and voids to endow his figure with a sense of movement as light plays across its surface and as the viewer's position changes. Integrating the human element with the abstract, the artist created an organic whole unlike anything that had been seen previously and one that remains striking and original today.

Contemporary figurative works often portray extreme states of mind, representing the individual with all his imperfections, often as a stand-in for mankind. The 1990 portrait head by Robert Arneson, *Wow Too* [P. 169], is a strong example. Trained as a ceramist on the West Coast, Arneson was influenced by the groundbreaking work of Peter Voulkos, who liberated clay from the limitations of its functional past. Arneson became one of the pioneering artists who swept aside the barrier between art and craft, managing in the process to offend, dismay, and delight both the sculptural world and that of traditional ceramics. Beginning in the 1970s, Arneson concentrated on portraiture, creating humorous, larger-than-life likenesses of himself, his friends, and artists he admired. Boldly modeled and brightly glazed, these portraits constitute sharp social and political commentary.

Arneson's work acquired a more serious bent after 1982 as he confronted matters of acute social concern, including racial tension and the dangers of a nuclear holocaust. His self-portraits took on heightened emotional power that spoke of the pain and frustration of the human condition. In *Wow Too,* completed less than two years before his death, Arneson did not shy away from depicting the physical effects of cancer. Leonardo da Vinci's observation that the eye is the window of the soul still has currency, and it is rare that a portrait hides the eyes of the sitter. By covering his own eyes with sunglasses, Arneson blocks access to his inner thoughts and directs the viewer's attention to his mouth. Here, the artist's long fight with cancer is memorialized in an agonizing cry that breaks through the cool detachment of his "pop" sunglasses.

Akio Takamori's sexually explicit and controversial heads have also expanded the limits of what is conventionally acceptable. Takamori received his training as a traditional potter in his native Japan. Although the vessel form continues to inform his work in slab-constructed porcelain, Takamori's art has undergone a profound transformation after nearly thirty years in America. Combining features of Eastern and Western art and thought as he explores human relationships—interpersonal, archetypal, social and historical—Takamori has devised a personal vocabulary that has increased the expressive potential of ceramic sculpture.

In the late 1980s, Takamori created a series of hollow busts with a new dynamic between inner and outer space. In the Chazens' 1991 *Eyes of a Young Woman* [P. 139], pairs of eyes proliferate on the figure. The artist envisions these as the eyes of other people in the subject's life,[1] but they may also be seen as representing the inner thoughts and fears that are

1
Takamori, personal communication, October 2004.

hidden behind the inscrutable public face. Fluid lines recalling those of Japanese calligraphy or woodcuts emphasize the contours of the head and eyes and create a three-dimensional stage on which the dramatic spectrum of human experience and emotions are played out. Object and subject revel in dualities—inside and out, drawing and form, male and female, union and separation—as the image on the vessel and its shape merge.

Ceramic artist Patti Warashina came of age during the 1960s under the influence of West Coast funk art, which drew inspiration from dada, surrealism, pop art, and Beat culture. Her *See No Evil* in the Chazen collection [P. 157], one of a series of low-fired, polychrome clay heads from 1993 (along with *Hear No Evil* and *Speak No Evil*), deals with the age-old image of three monkeys shielding their eyes, ears, and mouths. In this piece, however, two stylized hands, rather than covering the figure's eyes, intriguingly hold them open and reveal a second set of eyes above the first. Warashina's figure insists on dealing with reality, but it is the altered reality found in a dream. With the hollow form of traditional ceramic urns, *See No Evil* reflects the common notion of the human head as a vessel or receptacle for the spirit.

Some of the Chazens' strongest portrait heads have been executed in glass. The provocative German glass artist Erwin Eisch flouted taste and tradition when he coupled his technical mastery of the glass medium with an educated understanding of contemporary art and a vivid imagination. Heavily influenced by action painting, early pop art, and the German school of fantastic realism, Eisch rejected clear glass in favor of dark or opaque surfaces that he modeled and engraved. His silver-colored, blown-glass head *My Love to Anne Frank* [P. 74] was created as a monument against injustice and hate in response to an invitation from the American Interfaith Institute of Philadelphia in 1992. For this work, Eisch used a mold of Pablo Picasso's head as a blank canvas on which he engraved symbols of Anne Frank's life in order to "mull over, digest and regurgitate a collective memory of the Holocaust." He chose Picasso as a symbol of outspokenness against war's brutality and hate. Eisch wants viewers to look through his engravings "to see themselves reflected" and to experience the fragility of glass both metaphorically and physically. As a result, his unusual double portrait of Picasso and Anne Frank literalizes the triangulation between artist, subject, and viewer that operates in every portrait.

Swedish artist Bertil Vallien's sand-cast glass sculptures, notably his totems, boats and heads, abound with symbolic signs and allusions suggesting journeys into the mists of history and myth. Suspended in a dreamlike and mysterious ocean of glass, Vallien's enigmatic 1991 head entitled *Staircase* [P. 145] connects viewer and artist in a search for an innately powerful, spiritual light. The physical properties of glass make it the ideal vehicle for Vallien's ideas. He observes, "The simpler the form, the greater will be the emphasis on light—transforming the sculpture into cosmic matter—from space to the depths of the earth."

Staircase subverts the traditional mission of a portrait head and, instead of communicating the hidden state of the psyche, remains impassive, submerged in a sea of symbols, most prominently staircases, both large and small, representing escape. The undifferentiated head reflects the artist's focus on the universal rather than the individual and may be his manifestation of Jung's collective unconscious. In *Man and His Symbols,* Jung wrote, "It is the aim of the modern artist to give expression to his inner vision of man, to the spiritual background of life and the world." The golden head is a potent symbol in Vallien's pantheon of expressive archetypes.

The timeless imagery of Vallien's head resonates with the haunting portrait head created by Janusz Walentynowicz in his 1991 *Crossing* [P. 130]. However, Walentynowicz's naked, vulnerable figure represents a very different sensibility. Walentynowicz examines issues of identity through images that encourage us to reflect on ourselves more as individuals than as stand-ins for humanity. He lets us see his figure through a transparent mass of kiln-cast glass, suspended with an ambiguous facial expression that encourages us to formulate our own story for the figure from the few signs he gives us. The transparency of glass becomes a metaphor urging us to look past external signs of identity to see underlying emotional strata. "The traces of surface, color and texture both hold back and reveal clues. You can look past these external details of identity right into the scars and stress of experience, which are still evident and threatening internally though healed on the surface."[2]

2
Janusz Walentynowicz in an interview with Nannette V. Maciejunes, senior curator of the Columbus Museum of Art, *Glass Focus,* April/May 1995.

Hidden in the frenetic, beat-up glass casting of Hank Murta Adams's *Flagman* of 1988 [P. 121] is an intensely personal expression of the artist's anti-technological bent. The copper loops for eyes and mouth, the snake-like metal spikes of hair, and the swirling metal flag elements activate Adams's head. The red and green patinated copper extensions that encircle the torso give the figure its title and allude perhaps to the many invisible stop-and-go signals that inhibit everyday life. These suggestions of motion contrast strikingly with the ghostly, static quality of the glass.

Adams's working methods are uncompromising and painstaking; his figures survive a difficult birthing process to emerge stunned and somewhat alienated from their surroundings. The sandblasted torso of *Flagman* embodies the paradoxical combination of fragility and weight that is common to the human head and to glass. Although slightly translucent, this haunting work has little of glass's jewel-like quality. *Flagman,* simultaneously poignant and repellent, seems frozen in time and communicates little beyond a vacant expression, as if things were moving too swiftly to digest. Like many of the works the Chazens have collected, this is not an easily readable work that does the thinking for you—it is challenging, perplexing, and thoroughly absorbing.

Dan Dailey is a consummate glass artist who has worked glass in many different ways to create a wide range of effects. Using glass blowing for *Mephisto Man* [P. 64], Dailey embellishes the large-scale vessel form by applying color within the layers of glass and adding hot-glass surface decoration. Like each piece in his Face Vase series, *Mephisto Man* depicts a secondary motif, an angel, on the reverse side of the vase that relates to the identity of the subject. The streamlined elegance of the art deco period is reflected in this face vase with its elongated, angular features.

The glass heads of Polish-born Czeslaw Zuber bear the garish neon colors and in-your-face directness of graffiti. After breaking a block of optical crystal with a hammer, Zuber chisels, sandblasts, polishes, and paints the glass to bring forth heads that assert themselves with bright postmodern signs and symbols. The brassy aggressiveness of these heads may camouflage the artist's vulnerable inner poetry, and the open, teeth-bearing muzzles and mouths—a recurring leitmotif in Zuber's heads—may be there to bite, but perhaps also to fight off the bites of others. In *Mozart,* an allegorical portrait from 2000 [P. 96], Zuber creates a visual code in which Mozart stands for music itself. Zuber's raucously colorful musical notes aspire to the level of synesthesia in which musical stimuli may be perceived as sounds and sounds as color. In fact, the entire piece can be seen as a glass colorist's paean to the vitality of music and color experienced together.

There are many other important examples of figurative works in the Chazen collection, but it is fitting to end this exploration of heads with a masterpiece by the renowned Czech artists Stanislav Libenský and his wife Jaroslava Brychtová. The couple's fascination with the human head started in 1955 with *Head Bowl,* the first joint endeavor in their long and celebrated collaboration. Over the next half-century, they returned to the subject again and again.

In their pioneering artistic innovations in glass, Libenský and Brychtová absorbed, refined, and expanded upon earlier modernist art movements, cubism in particular, creating a balance between geometric abstraction and figuration. The Chazens' *Cross Head* [P. 107] was completed in 1994. A striking ruby-colored geometric composition, this sculpture masterfully reveals the artists' depth of understanding of glass and the mold-melted technique they perfected. To animate *Cross Head,* Libenský and Brychtová cantilevered the block-like head over a thin base, establishing a dynamic equilibrium that endows the work with a sense of fragility that softens its angular forms. The play of light upon and within its structure modulates the piece from the inside out; under different light conditions and from different viewing positions, *Cross Head* can transmute from a vibrant, glowing ruby red to a somber leaden black. These manifestations of inner light enliven the sculpture and endow it with complexity and mystery.

The figurative works in the Chazen collection affirm that the first priority of art, whatever the medium, is to address concepts and ideas. Through the prominent and recurring motif of the head, many of the artists in the collection inquire into the ambiguous, fluid nature of personal identity and the individual's place in society. Running the full range, from the lighthearted to the deeply moving, their creations are adventurous in spirit, honest, and compelling, reflecting the Chazens' passion for life as well as for collecting.

Jennifer Scanlan

ILLUMINATING VISION: LIGHT IN ABSTRACT GLASS SCULPTURE

Many of the glass artists in the Chazen collection consciously manipulate light in their creations, exploiting the particular qualities of their materials and the potential in their chosen glassworking techniques to capture or reflect light, to mute or intensify color, to create or dissolve form. Their sculptures interact with the environment, changing according to the kind and amount of light available and transforming themselves as the viewer shifts positions. Light adds a transitory and participatory element, making the viewer's experience of these works both interactive and elusive.

Abstract sculpture is a study of visual elements—spatial relations, volume, form, color, and texture. Light puts all of these elements into play, emphasizing, distorting, even undermining the viewer's visual impressions and forcing him or her to move beyond perceived reality. Abstraction provides a direct link to the viewer's thoughts or feelings, bypassing the preformed associations that accompany the perception of recognizable imagery. Light can serve as a channel of access to the subconscious, inviting meditation or direct emotional response. Focusing on the interaction of light with abstract glass sculptures reveals their many layers of visual and conceptual complexity.

For artists who work with a limited palette of color and form, the manipulation of light can suggest the intricacy that underlies the simplicity. Steven Weinberg's untitled work from 1983 [P. 79] comes from a series of minimalist-inspired geometric pieces that he produced in the early 1980s. His use of brilliantly clear lead crystal, the surface treated by sandblasting and polishing, both allows us to view the cube's interior and prevents us from doing so. The light plays off the surface—glinting on polished round ends, glowing softly as it touches on the sandblasted interiors. The work, a straightforward assemblage of one basic repeated geometric form, is rendered complex and boundless.

Maria Lugossy's *Laminated Glass Sculpture* from 1986 [P. 99] similarly calls on the reflective qualities of light to suggest an interior larger than the exterior. Lugossy's use of glass plates, stacked and laminated together, and of the pyramidal form, gives the sculpture a sense of solidity and stability; at the same time light, entering into the green-glass depths of her piece, renders it ephemeral. Through the reflection of the form within itself, physical boundaries are dissolved and infinite space is circumscribed. Light here acts as sculptor, recreating endlessly the shiny precise sides and angles as well as the sandblasted erosion that eats at the core of the pyramid.

Like Lugossy, Tom Patti uses laminated glass in his *Solarized Blue* from 1986 [P. 98]. The veil-like boundaries between the layers of glass serve to delineate motion and the displacement of matter. The air bubble inside the piece is defined by the amount of light that passes through the cube and the gleam of light reflected on the bubble's curved side. The result is a contained image that uses subtle gradations of tone to make quiet impact and encourage contemplation.

Howard Ben Tré's *Second Flask* from 1989 [P. 117] also uses the passage of light under the surface to draw the viewer's attention to the interior. The title defines the piece as a container. Head on, the work traces the silhouette of a chemist's flask, although the piece is open at front and back, rendering it nonfunctional; from the side, however, the interior is visible, and it is apparent that the work is a container of light. The brass that lines the sculpture's cavities is plated with gold leaf, visible only through the murkiness of the thick glass exterior. The gold absorbs and reflects light, giving the piece an inner glow. Ben Tré's casting process leads to bubbles and fissures that, along with the rough surface and milky cast, freeze the light within.

Like Ben Tré, Stanislav Libenský and Jaroslava Brychtová cast their glass sculptures. Rather than directing the viewer inward, however, in their 1989 work *The Column* [P. 166] Libenský and Brychtová use the optical qualities of clear glass to reflect and crazily fragment the surrounding environment. In the manner of a prism, the angles and planes of *The Column* bend rays of light, causing images from the sculpture's exterior to appear inside it in unexpected ways.

Jon Kuhn takes this prismatic effect to an extreme in his complex configurations of colored and clear glass cubes. The play of reflective light within his 1992 sculpture *Orchid Spring* [P. 122] is a direct result of his explorations of Eastern mysticism. Kuhn explains: "Through meditation we find the universe within." Kuhn's cubes, in fact, seem to contain an entire universe, created by, and celebrating, light. He uses two kinds of glass—nonreflective borosilicate and brilliant lead fluoride—to manipulate light in different ways. The cubes (and cubes within cubes) both absorb the light, creating an inner glow, and reflect it, repeating the complicated reticulation at the core of the piece in an endless variety of patterns.

While in Jon Kuhn's sculpture the play of light happens on the interior, in William Carlson's work *Pragnanz Series #8* of 1987 [P. 138], light interacts with the exterior. The polished granite reflects light, while the beveled glass appears both opaque and transparent, depending on the position of the viewer and the way in which light hits the surface. The three sections of the sculpture are positioned obliquely, and the glass appears and disappears as the viewer travels around the piece. Like Kuhn, Carlson incorporates colored glass, both clear and opaque, which here serves as a segue from the impenetrable granite to the clear glass. Carlson's work is all about angles: both the physical angles describing his glass and granite forms, brought forcibly to our attention through the violence of their intersection, and, more subtly, the light angles—angles of refraction and reflection—that create volume and void.

Mary Shaffer's *Hanging Series Water—White #3* from 1991 [P. 141] also uses the disappearing effect of clear glass to create a work more about void than about form. Though she uses the slumped glass technique, heating the glass in a kiln until it is shaped by its own weight, light passes quickly through the clear glass of the finished piece, leaving only the faintest of traces, so that the sculpture appears to be weightless, immaterial, a shadow rather than an actual object.

While many artists in the Chazen collection use clear glass for its particular manipulation of light—reflecting and refracting images, creating and dissolving form—others focus on the interaction of light with colored glass. Optical scientists tell us that color is a product of light, the result of the way in which our eyes detect differing qualities of projected or reflected light. Many glass artists in the Chazen collection manipulate the passage of light through their works to create soft subtle shades or hues of exceptional vividness. The dynamic interaction of light with color creates movement and mood in their pieces.

Susan Stinsmuehlen-Amend's *Stained Glass Windows* of 1986–87 [PP. 162–3] carefully control light for both functional and aesthetic reasons. The artist's limited use of color allows for the passage of enough light to ensure that the interior artwork is well lit. She selected three kinds of glass to affect the clarity of light: industrial glass to create areas of flat color; European hand-blown glass panels that shift gradually from milky white to clear, creating delicate shadows as if shaded in by pencil; and hand-blown roundels that describe circles of light changing in intensity according to the thickness of the glass. The uneven refraction of light created by the irregularity of the hand-blown glass softens and distorts the edges of color fields, contrasting with the bright industrial panels. Finally, the lead lines show up as black shadows, which both create a structure (physically and visually) and, through their varying thicknesses, add a graphic element.

A number of artists focus on a single color to explore effects of light and transparency. Lino Tagliapietra's sculpture from 1999, *Red Dinosaur #705* [P. 69], is a study of one shade of red and the patterns achieved by the passage of light. A recognized master of Venetian glassblowing, Tagliapietra has reinforced the graceful form and brilliant color achieved in the blowing process by engraving the surface of the vessel. Light coming through the vessel highlights vertical stripes (created by thin glass canes applied to the hot glass before blowing) that echo the work's curves, almost as if the light itself were causing the belly to swell. Light plays over thin horizontal cuts on the surface, outlining the piece in a hazy glow and rendering its elegant form dynamic.

Stanislav Libenský and Jaroslava Brychtová's *Cross Head* of 1994 [P. 107], like Tagliapietra's *Red Dinosaur,* is a solid deep red. Without light, the piece stands as a cubist composition of blocks and angles. When light passes through the sculpture, however, it becomes a dynamic and nuanced form, revealing inner junctures, subtle shadings, and a glowing core. The deep, almost black red, heats up to a brilliant vermilion, becoming an incandescent orange at the edges and along inside seams. Like the human head that it represents abstractly, *Cross Head,* simple on the outside, has inner workings of startling complexity.

Mark Peiser's *Polychrome Fan* from 1983 [P. 92] also presents a range of colors. Unlike *Cross Head,* in which color effects are created by the varying thicknesses of and points of contact between different parts, *Polychrome Fan* is solid. Colors change according to the light source and the viewer's position. Part of a series called Innerspace, this piece represents one of Peiser's first examinations of the optical qualities of cast glass. "I didn't want the surface to be anything like a barrier, but rather to serve as an invisible interface from one world to another."[1] Through painstaking technical experimentation, Peiser explored colors and flow patterns to achieve a work that goes beyond the physical manifestations of material and technique, allowing the viewer to connect more directly with the emotions or thought behind the work.

Harvey Littleton's work from 1979, *Triple Loop* [P. 160], similarly grew out of technical experimentation, using an overlay technique to create tubes of brilliant color. In this piece, the core of each loop is a pure, bright pink. The lead crystal that encases the core gives the color a shiny gloss with the hard, wet look of lacquer. At the same time, the encasement fragments the color as refracted light slices the core into slivers of color that break apart and reform as the viewer moves around the piece.

1
As quoted in Dan Klein, "Compositions in Glass: The Art of Mark Peiser," in *Looking Within: Mark Peiser, the Art of Glass* (Ashville, N. C.: Asheville Art Museum, 2003), 11.

Dominick Labino's *Emergence,* from the same period [P. 158], explores the colored inner core on a more subtle scale. The delicate bubbles that are contained within the piece overlap and fold in on themselves. The gentle play of light through varying layers of color is enhanced by the faint gold sheen on the surface of one of the interior bubbles. Light reflecting off of this diaphanous glimmer gives the piece an ethereal quality, as if formed of air and light.

Many of the glass artists represented in the Chazen collection use a range of colors in their works. In their pieces, light is often an animating agent, increasing or muting contrasts, combining two colors to create a third, acting as a living paintbrush. Joel Philip Myers adds color to his pieces using glass marquetry, adhering sheets of colored glass to clear blown glass vessels. In *Flattened Vessel* from 1988 [P. 89], the clear glass serves as a curved canvas, allowing colors to undulate over its surface. Patches of color reflect or absorb light according to their tone and position. As colors overlap, they change or darken; seen from the opposite side, they become unfocused, distorted.

Marvin Lipofsky also uses the vessel form to enhance his colors and their interaction with light. In *Pilchuck Summer Series #4* from 1988–89 [P. 153], colors change in intensity and feeling from outside to inside. Like Myers, Lipofsky adds his colors to the hot surface of the mold-blown vessel. After creating a series on location (in this example at the Pilchuck School of Glass in Stanford, Washington), Lipofsky returns to his studio in Berkeley, California, to complete his pieces. He sandblasts the outer surface, which captures light softly. He also cuts slits and holes into the form, which allows the slicker, shinier interior to show through with more vivid colors and a "hotter" quality of light. Lipofsky is inspired in his palette by his surroundings. In this piece, colors that seem to have the coolness of a Northwest summer on the outside have all of the fire of a glassblowing furnace on the inside.

While Lipofsky's round form seems to hold fire within, Dale Chihuly's *Macchia Basket* from 1986 [P. 159] blossoms open in a celebration of color and light. His dappled blues and pinks recall the impressionists' explorations of dissolving light and color. Light moving through the vessel creates stipples and reflections, making it hard to distinguish what has been achieved by permanent color and what by transitory light. The movement of light on the shiny, undulating surface recalls the play of light on water, giving the piece a sense of motion.

Klaus Moje's 1992 plate *Untitled #27* [P. 155] also uses light for a painterly effect. Although his pieces have been compared to abstract expressionist paintings in their seemingly spontaneous style, they are actually created through a complex and lengthy process that the artist has developed in order to combine sections of kiln-formed glass mosaics with glass canes of pure color. The light shining through the translucent forms makes the lines of color shimmer and dance.

By incorporating light as an active component in their abstract glass sculptures, the artists represented in the Chazen collection add resonance to their work, both visually and conceptually. Taking advantage of the properties of light and its interaction with materials, surfaces, and colors, they expand the physical characteristics of their work to include interiors larger than exteriors, forms that appear and disappear, colors that move and transform. Through light they alter the viewer's perception, stimulating ideas and emotions, making light a conduit from the material to the immaterial. They sculpt with light as well as glass, to illuminate in all senses.

All measurements are given in inches.
Height precedes width precedes depth.

GERHARD RICHTER
Abstract Painting No. 623,
1987
oil on canvas
100 X 100
Art © Gerhard Richter,
Photo © Christie's Images Inc.,
1996

JACQUES LIPCHITZ
Tête (Head), 1915
cast bronze
24 x 9½ x 9⅝
Art © 2004 Artists Rights
Society (ARS), New York/
ADAGP Paris; Photo © Christie's
Images Inc., 1990

DONALD LIPSKI
Pilchuck #90-21, 1990
slumped glass, fry basket
24 x 7 x 6

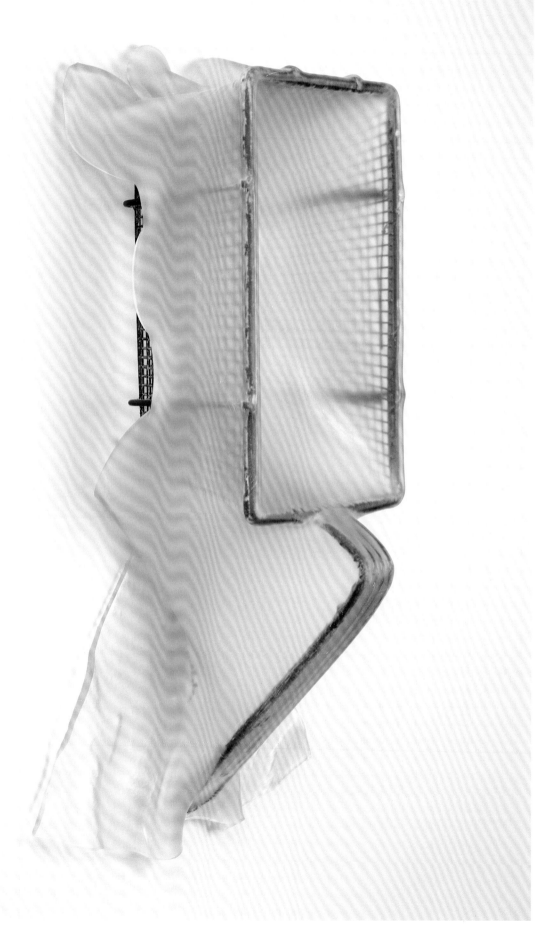

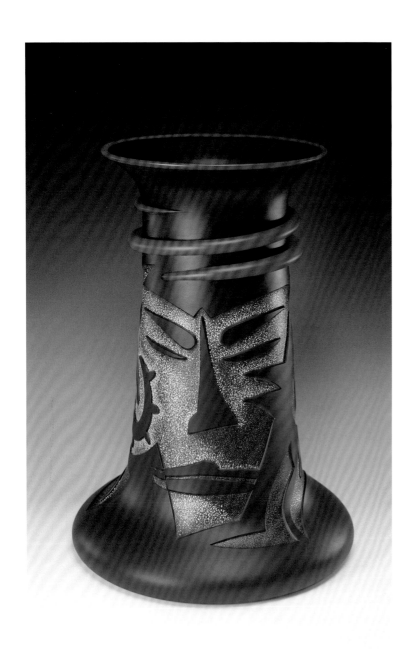

DAN DAILEY
Mephisto Man, 1990
blown cobalt blue glass
with red wrap and multi-
colored enamel painting
17 ¾ x 12 ¾ (diameter)

JOAQUÍN
TORRES-GARCÍA
Constructivo a Cinco
Colores con Locomotora
Azul, 1943
oil on board
22 X 27

SYDNEY CASH
Untitled Red /
White Form, 1988–93
slumped glass,
plate glass, wire
13 ½ x 9 ½ x 6 ½

MANUEL NERI
Remaking of Mary Julia
No. 2, 2002
bronze, mixed media
63 x 29 x 15

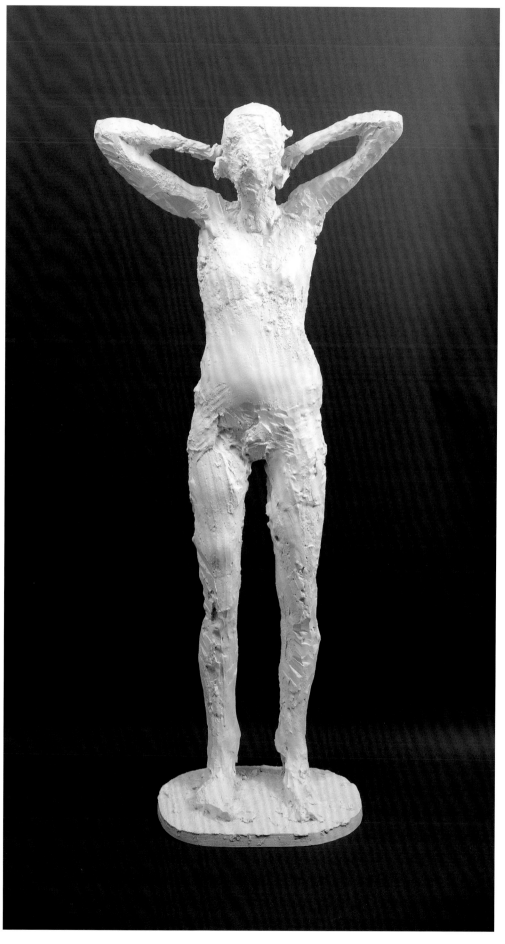

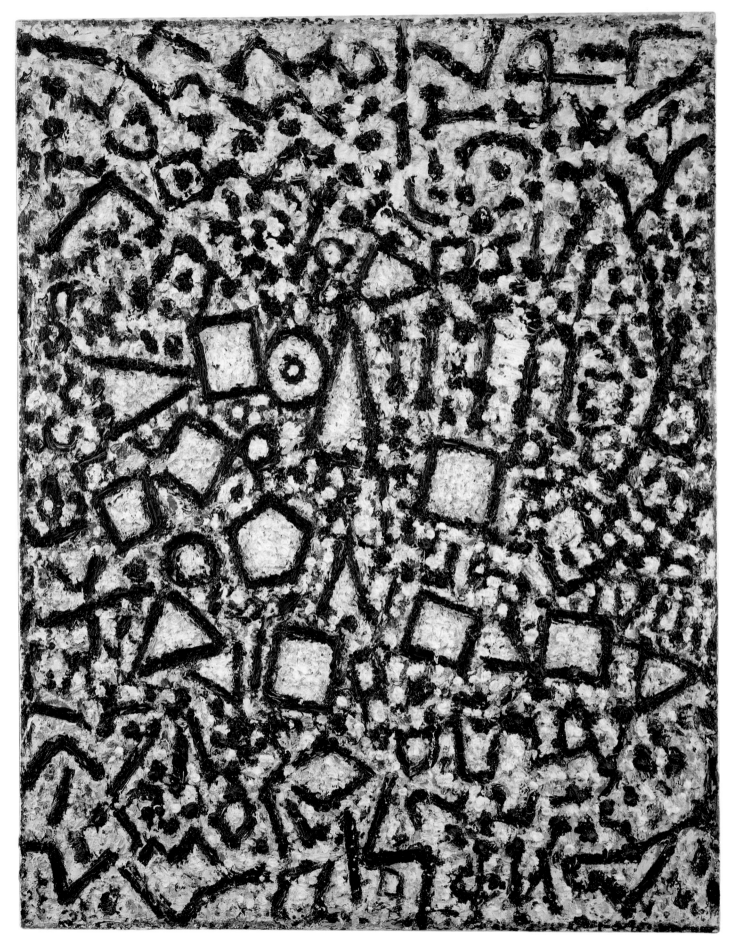

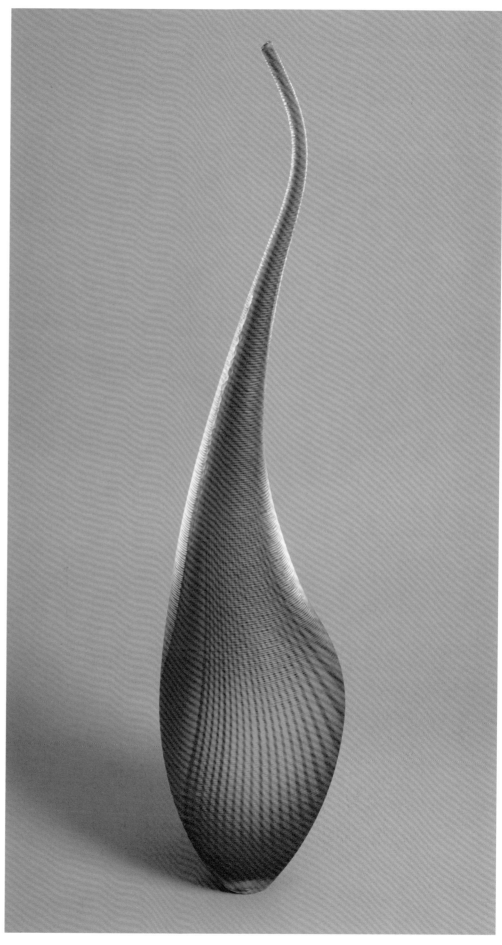

RICHARD
POUSETTE-DART
Myth of the Calyx, 1979
oil on linen
42 x 33

LINO TAGLIAPIETRA
Red Dinosaur #705, 1999
blown glass, inciso, battuto
41 ¼ x 9 ½ x 6 ¼

JAMES WATKINS
Two Bottles, 1991
cast glass
11 ¾ x 6 x 4

LARRY RIVERS
Last Civil War Veteran,
1962
oil on board
30 ⅛ x 22 ⅞

WILLIAM MORRIS
Standing Stone, 1984
mold-blown cased glass
31 X 13 X 7

GEORGE GROSZ
Nude, 1916
pencil on paper
22 X 19
Art © Estate of George Grosz/
Licensed by VAGA, New York, NY

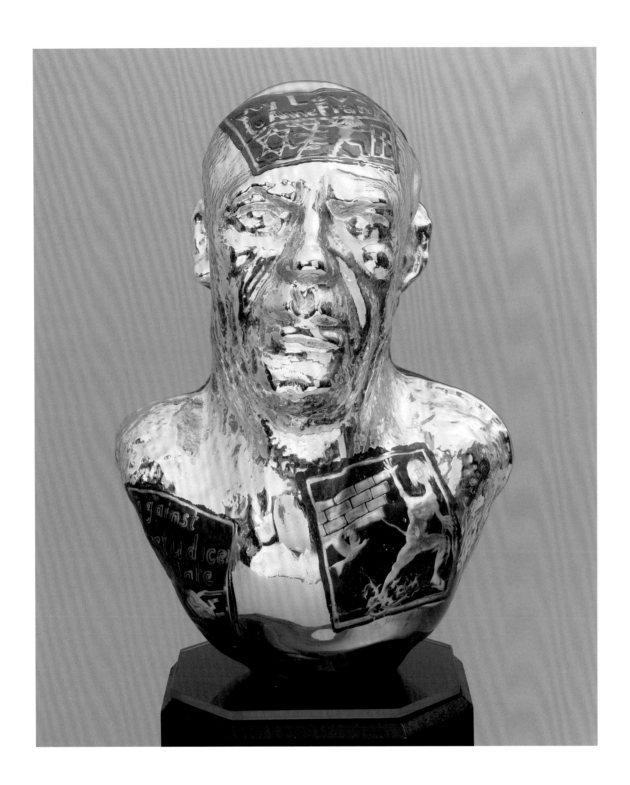

ERWIN EISCH
My Love to Anne Frank,
1992
mold-blown glass, fired-on
enamels
20 x 14 x 8

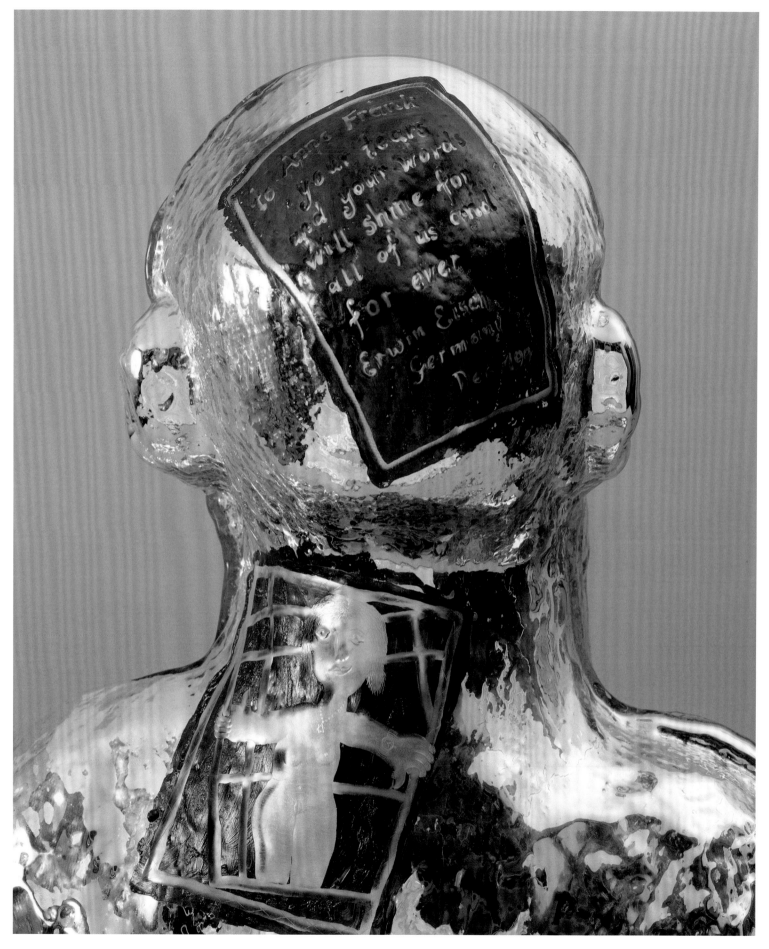

ALEXANDER CALDER
Mountain Range, 1965
gouache on paper
29 X 42
© Estate of Alexander Calder/
Artists Rights Society (ARS),
New York

Calder

65

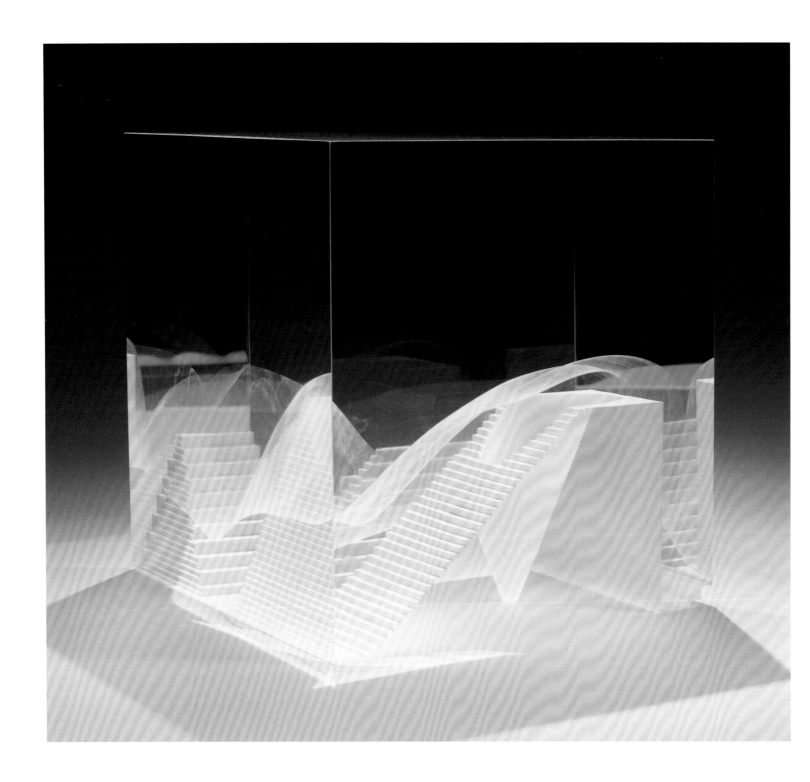

STEVEN I. WEINBERG
Cast Crystal Cube, 1990
cast and sandblasted glass
8 x 8 x 8

STEVEN I. WEINBERG
Untitled, 1983
cast, faceted, and
sandblasted glass
5 x 6 ¼ x 6 ¼

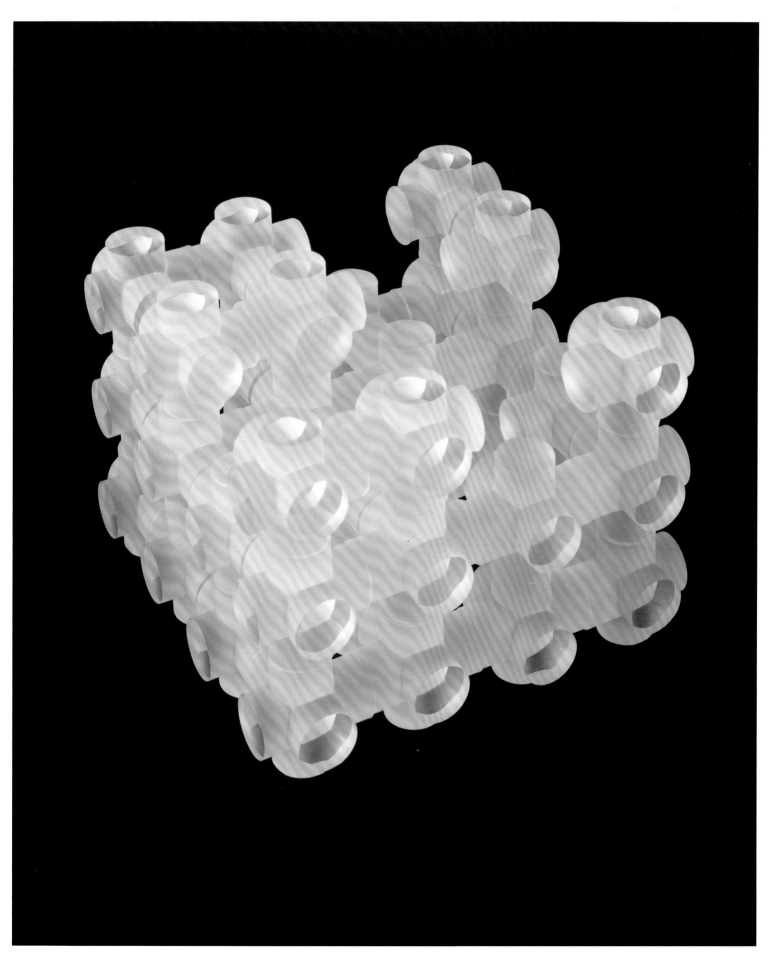

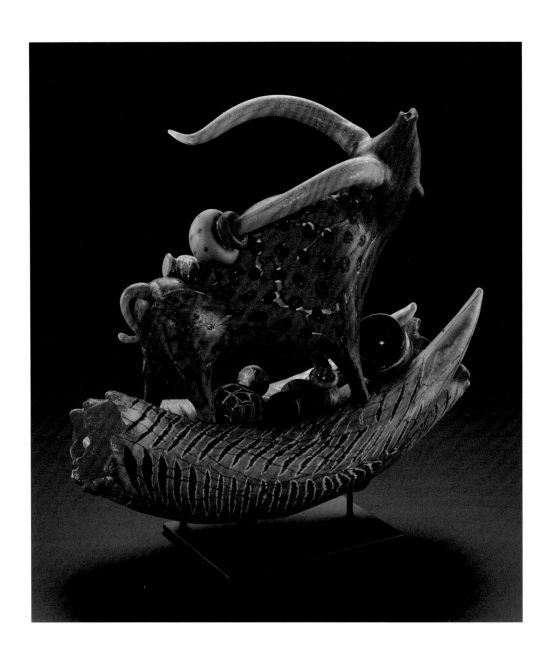

WILLIAM MORRIS
Raft, 1998
handblown and sculpted
glass
18 x 18 x 9

SANDRO CHIA
Horseman in Front of
the Sea, 1986
acrylic on canvas
86½ x 78½
Art © Sandro Chia/Licensed
by VAGA, New York, NY

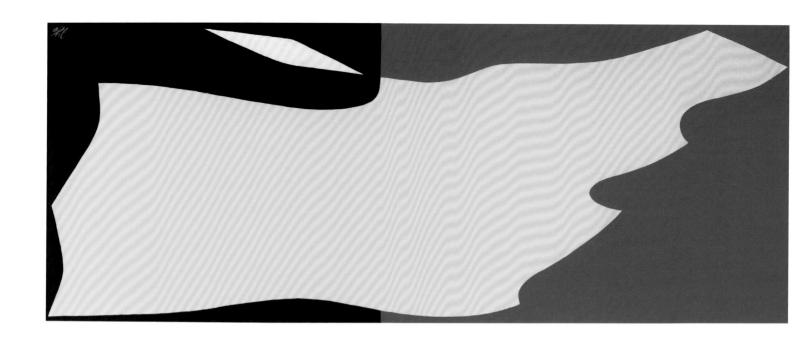

JACK YOUNGERMAN
Bridgehampton, 1969
acrylic on canvas
19 x 48
Art © Jack Youngerman/
Licensed by VAGA, New York, NY

KARLA TRINKLEY
White Arrow Bowl, 1991
pâte de verre
12 x 12 ½ (diameter)

JEAN DUBUFFET
Danse Elance, 1971
acrylic paint on Klegecell
111 x 177 x 1¼
© 2004 Artists Rights Society
(ARS), New York/ADAGP Paris

MILTON AVERY
Belle, 1941
gouache on paper
24 x 18
© Milton Avery Trust/Artists
Rights Society (ARS), New York

CAPPY THOMPSON
Fiddler, 1991
blown glass, reverse
painted in enamels
24 x 14 (diameter)

GINNY RUFFNER
Another Pretty Face, 1993
flameworked glass and
mixed media
15 X 20 X 11

JOEL PHILIP MYERS
Flattened Vessel, 1988
blown glass
13 ¾ x 18 ½ x 3 ½

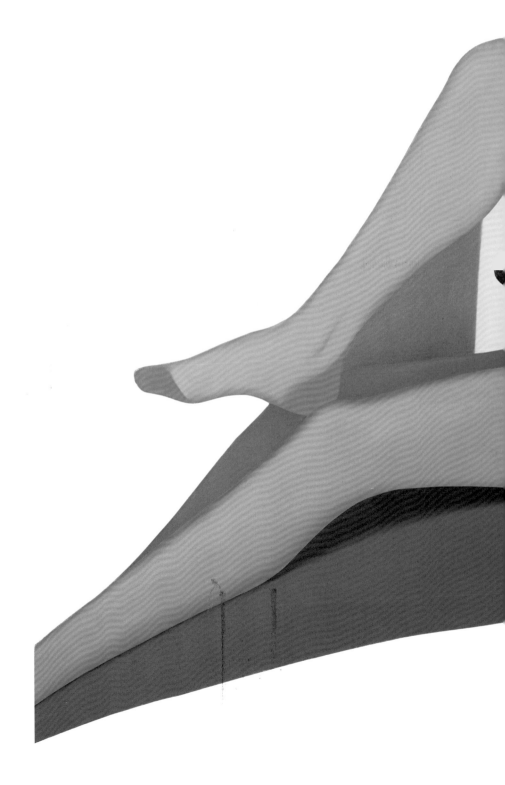

TOM WESSELMANN
Stockinged Nude with
Fishbowl, 1982
oil on shaped canvas
48 x 66
Art © Tom Wesselmann/
Licensed by VAGA, New York, NY

MARK PEISER
Polychrome Fan, 1983
cast glass
8 x 4 x 3 ½

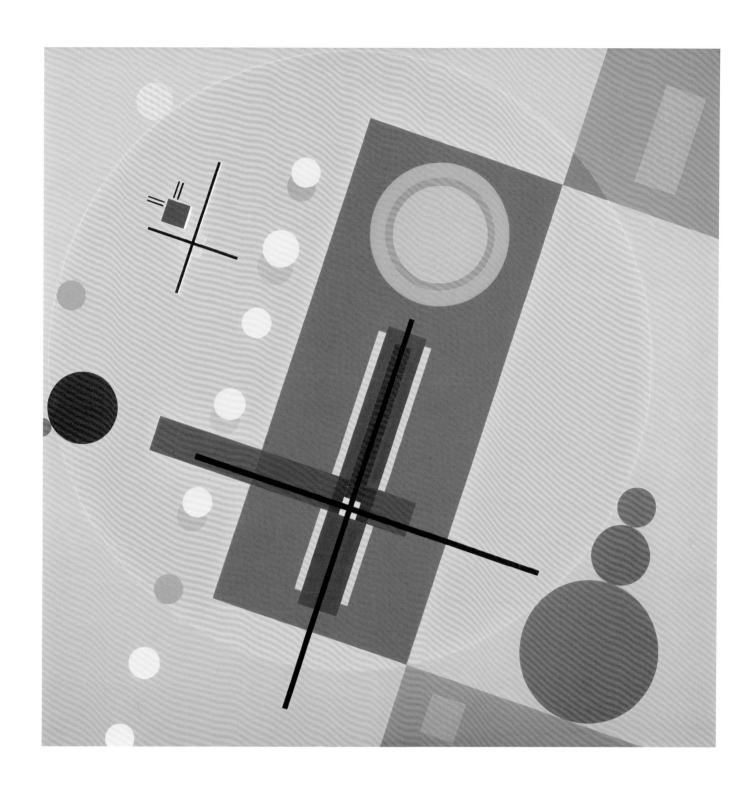

ED GARMAN
Untitled #285, 1942
oil on Masonite
30 x 30

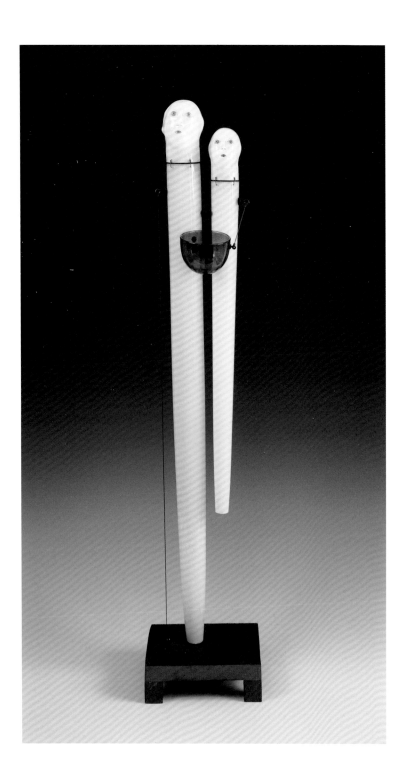

FLORA C. MACE AND
JOEY KIRKPATRICK
Vision with Likeness, 1985
hand- and mold-blown
glass, slate, steel,
enamels
35 × 5 × 5

JOHN McLAUGHLIN
Untitled, 1953
oil on Masonite
38 ⅛ × 31 ¾
Photo © Christie's Images
Inc., 1997

CZESLAW ZUBER
Mozart, 1992
fractured, cut, and
enameled crystal
21 X 12 X 11

HANS HOFMANN
Untitled, 1950
oil on canvas
60 x 40
© 2004 Estate of Hans
Hofmann/Artists Rights
Society (ARS), New York

TOM PATTI
Solarized Blue, 1986
stacked, fused, blown and
polished glass
3½ x 3½ x 3½

MARIA LUGOSSY
Laminated Glass Sculpture,
1986
laminated glass
4 X 7 X 7

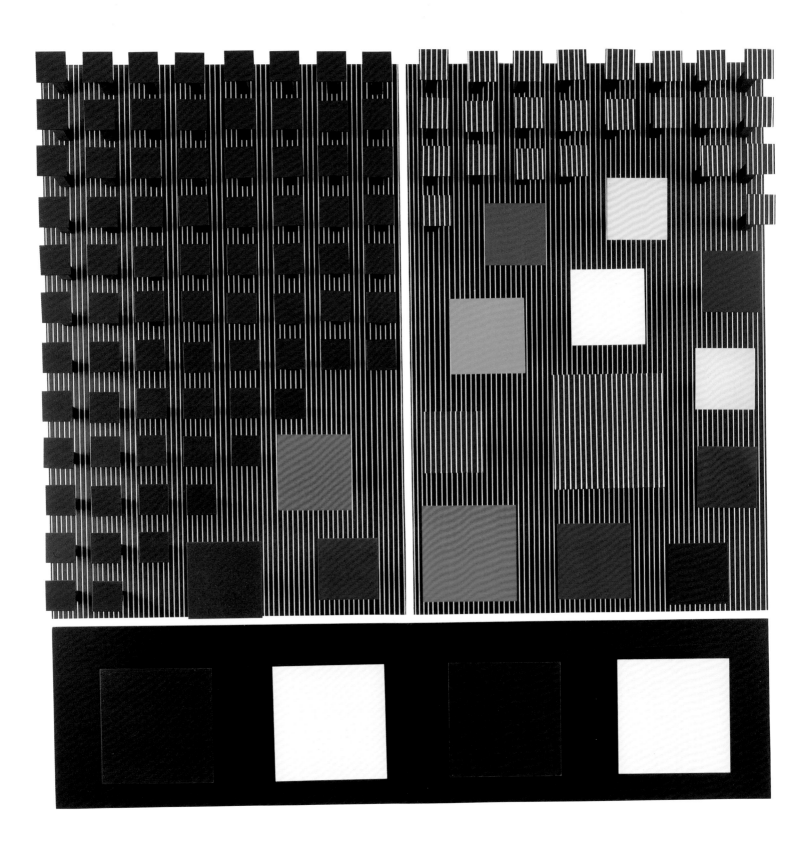

JESÚS RAFAEL SOTO   DAVID REEKIE
Diagonal Virtue, 1985   *Happy,* 1987
mixed media   cast glass
40 ½ x 40 ½ x 6 ½   14 x 9 ½ x 6
© 2004 Artists Rights Society
(ARS), New York/ADAGP Paris

FRANK STELLA
Double Scramble, 1978
Liquitex on canvas
69 ¼ x 138 ¼
© 2004 Frank Stella/Artists
Rights Society (ARS), New York

ANTHONY CARO
Mister, 1998–2000
stoneware with wood-
fired surface
31½ x 13½ x 9

JEAN DUBUFFET
Inspection du Territoire,
1974
acrylic on canvas
70¾ x 55
© 2004 Artists Rights Society
(ARS), New York/ADAGP Paris

LOUISE NEVELSON
Mirror Shadow xxxxv,
1987
wood, paint
46 x 33 x 3
© 2004 Estate of Louise
Nevelson/Artists Rights Society
(ARS), New York

**JAROSLAVA
BRYCHTOVÁ AND
STANISLAV LIBENSKÝ**
Cross Head, **1994**
cast glass
33 x 23 x 6

ROY LICHTENSTEIN
Two Figures, 1978
oil and Magna on canvas
36 x 48
© Estate of Roy Lichtenstein

MARY SHAFFER
Wall Treasures II, 1993
slumped glass, metal,
wood
28 x 28 x 7

PAUL STANKARD
*Spring Beauty with Spirits
under the Earth*, 1986
flameworked and
encased glass
5 x 2 ½ x 2 ½

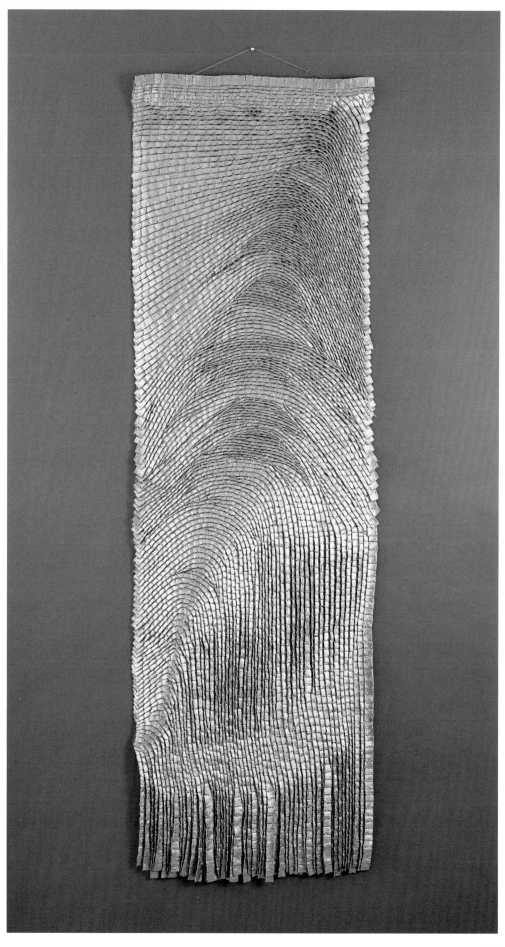

RICHARD
POUSETTE-DART
Forms: Transcendental,
1950
gouache on panel
24 x 19 ½

OLGA DE AMARAL
Umbra 17, **1999**
fiber, gold leaf, acrylic
62 x 20

LUCIO BUBACCO
Calice di Apollo (Apollo's
Chalice), 1998
flameworked glass
14 ½ x 9 x 5

KYOHEI FUJITA
Plum Blossom (six-sided
box), 1987
mold-blown glass,
decorated with foil,
colored glass chips
5 x 9 (diameter)

HOWARD BEN TRÉ
*Bearing Figure with Beak
Sprouted Vessel,* 1996
cast soda lime glass,
Canadian black granite
18 x 14 ½ x 14

HOWARD BEN TRÉ
Second Flask, 1989
cast glass, brass, gold leaf
71 x 19 x 18

In the background are works
by Philip Baldwin and Monica
Guggisberg (far left) and
Mel Kendrick (center).

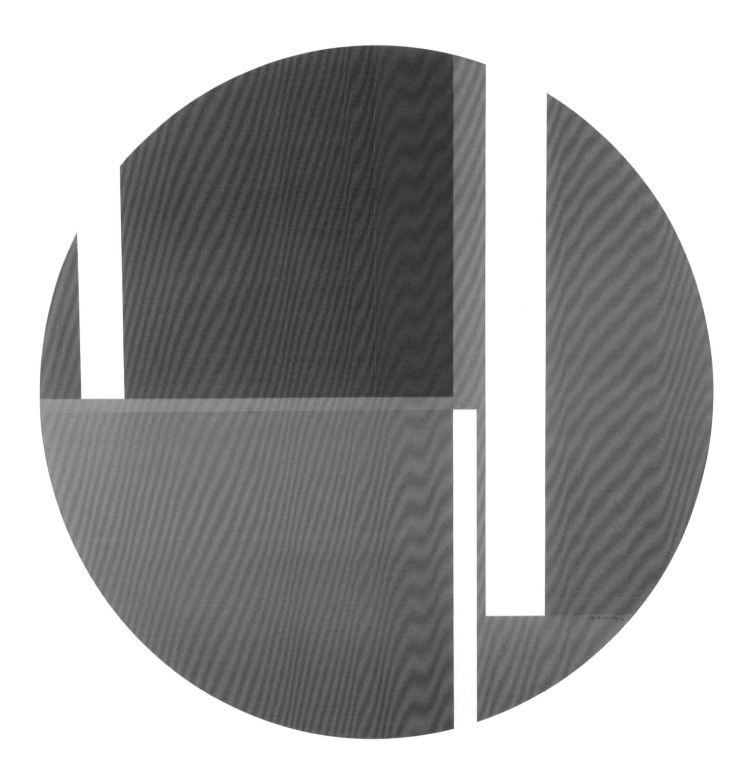

ILYA BOLOTOWSKY
Red Tondo, 1973
acrylic on canvas
39 ½ (diameter)
Art © Estate of Ilya
Bolotowsky/Licensed by
VAGA, New York, NY

WILLIAM MORRIS
Trophy, 1999
hand-blown and sculpted
glass, metal
33 x 30 x 14 (including
wall panel)

118

AL HELD
Untitled, 1960
acrylic on canvas
60 x 42
Art © Al Held/Licensed by
VAGA, New York, NY

HANK MURTA
ADAMS
Flagman, 1988
cast glass, metal
32 x 22 x 10

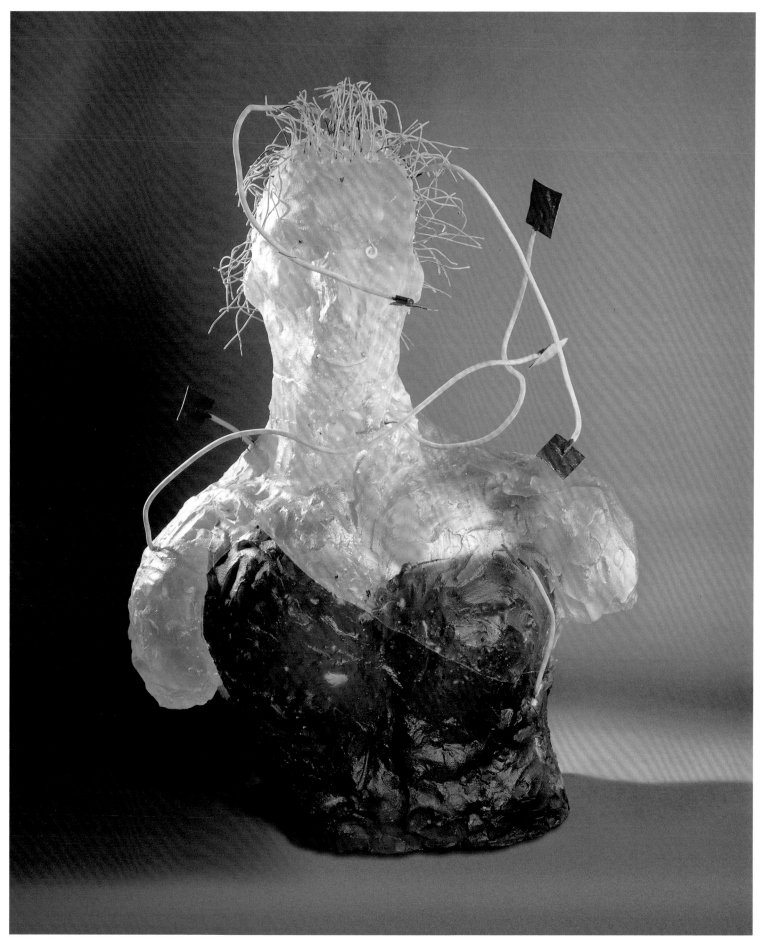

JON KUHN
Orchid Spring, 1992
bonded optical crystal
9 ¾ x 9 ¾ x 9 ¾ (cube);
13 ¾ x 12 ½ x 12 ½
(as installed)

BURGOYNE DILLER
First Theme, 1962
oil on canvas
42 x 42
© Estate of Burgoyne Diller/
Licensed by VAGA, New York, NY

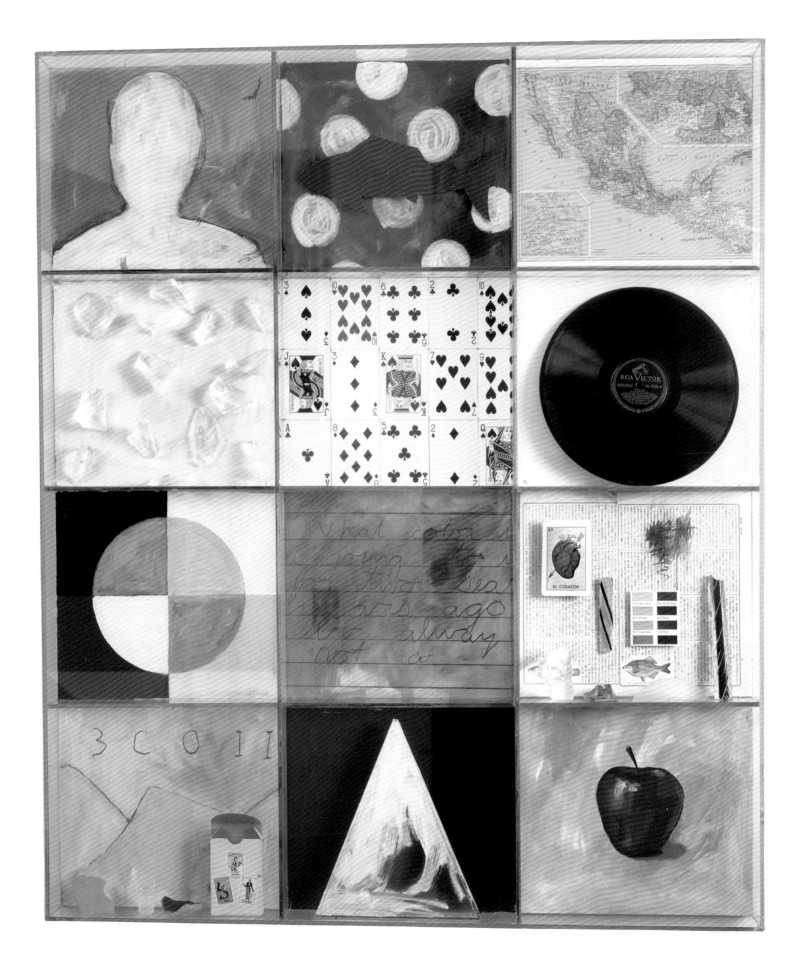

THERMAN STATOM
Serenata, 1993
painted and assembled
glass and found objects
42 ½ x 36 x 3 ½

MARY VAN CLINE
Fuchsia House Sculpture,
1984
cast and cut glass, photo-
sensitive glass, flame-
worked ladder, paint
19 x 9 x 3

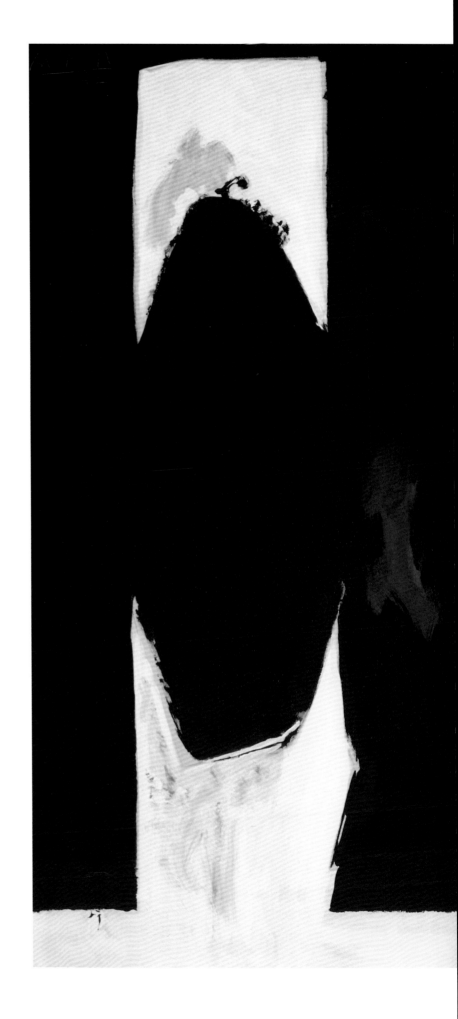

ROBERT MOTHERWELL
Elegy to the Spanish
Republic #125, 1972
acrylic with pencil and
charcoal on canvas
86 x 120
© Dedalus Foundation, Inc./
Licensed by VAGA, New York, NY

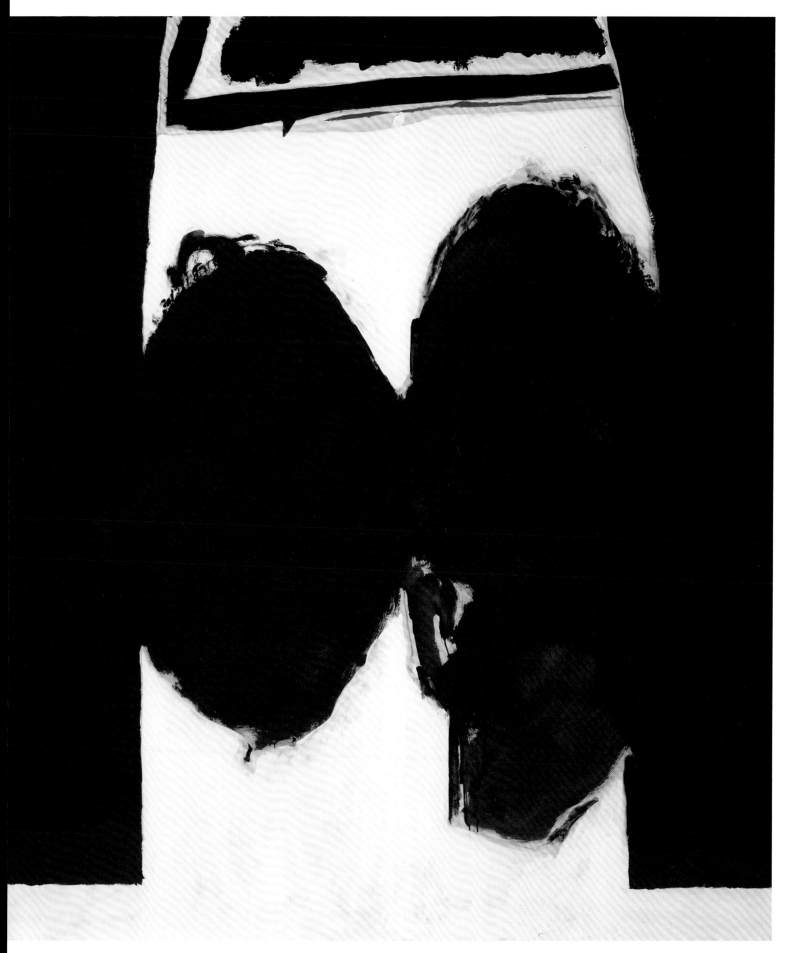

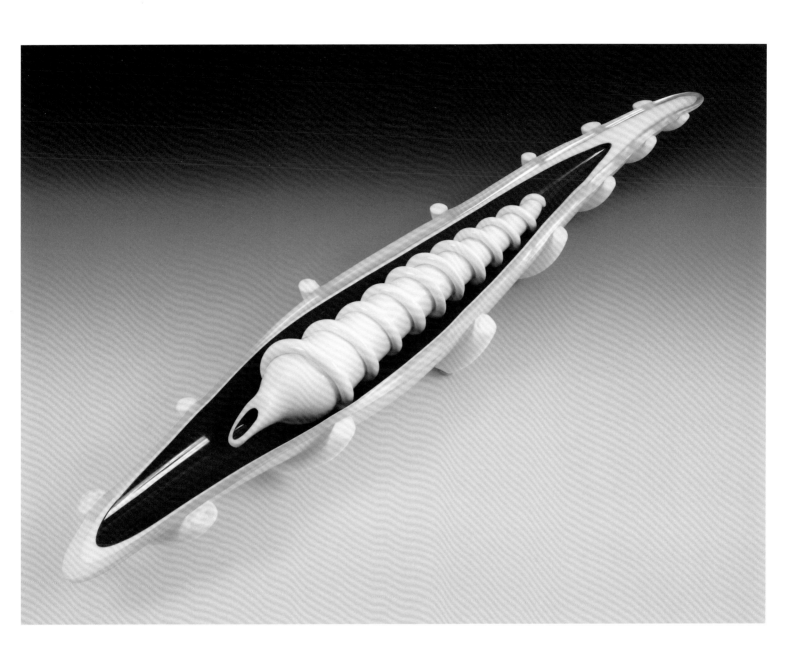

MARY MERKEL-HESS
Orange/Orange, 2000
reed and paper
39 x 32 x 24

STEVE TOBIN
Boat, ca. 1989
blown glass
5 x 8 x 43 (length)

JANUSZ
WALENTYNOWICZ
Crossing, 1991
cast glass
26 x 32 x 5½

ANN WOLFF
Spider Woman, ca. 1989
blown and acid-etched
glass, metal
32 x 23 x 13

DAVID HOCKNEY
The Sixteenth V.N.
Painting, 1992
oil on canvas
36 x 48

MICHAEL LUCERO
*Seated Man with Heart
on Face/Ohr Hair
(Pre-Columbus)*, 1991
hand-built earthenware
with glazes
19 x 10 x 10

DANIEL CLAYMAN
Ripple, 1999
pâte de verre, metal
11½ x 24 x 18½

RICHARD
POUSETTE-DART
Grael of Light, 1966–67
oil on canvas
60 x 60

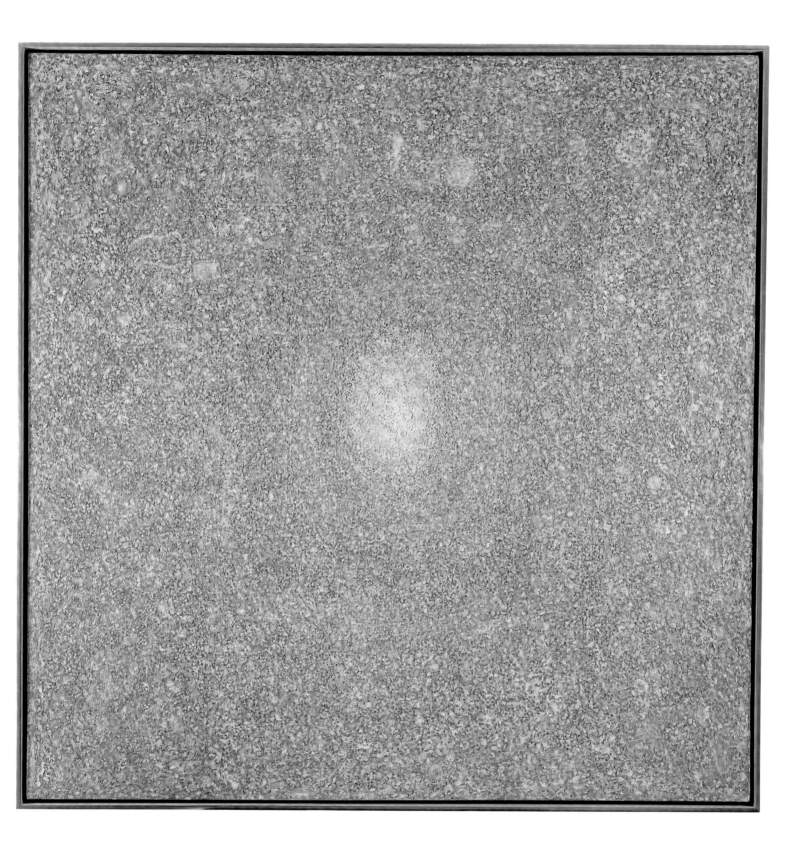

HARVEY K.
LITTLETON
Implied Movement, **1986**
glass
46 x 23 x 14 (as installed);
4–5 (diameter range)

DAN DAILEY
Chandelier, **1998–99**
pâte de verre; fused,
slumped, mold-formed,
sandblasted and acid-
polished borosilicate rods;
24 electric lamps; cast and
patinated bronze; steel
and aluminum structure;
gold plating; anodizing;
flameworked elements
37 x 42 x 21

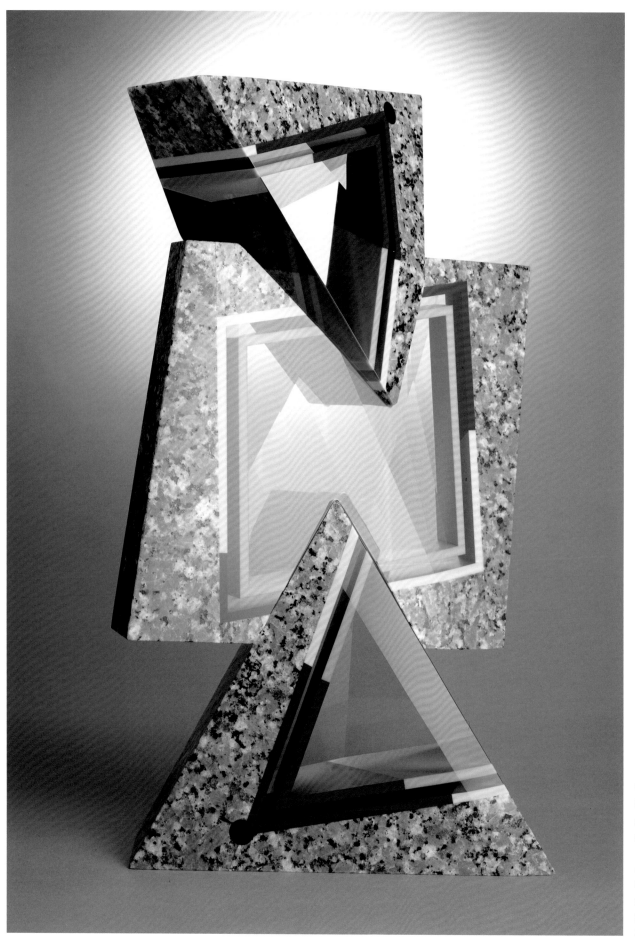

WILLIAM CARLSON
Pragnanz Series #8, 1987
glass, granite
23 x 12 x 6

AKIO TAKAMORI
Eyes of a Young Woman,
1991
porcelain, glaze
25 x 16 x 9

DALE CHIHULY
Indian Blanket Cylinder,
1987
blown glass, surface
decoration
12 ¼ x 8 ½ (diameter)

MARY SHAFFER
Hanging Series Water—
White #3, 1991
slumped glass, wire
24 x 24 x 5

ITALO SCANGA
Untitled, 1986
charcoal and gouache
on paper
23½ x 17¾

ALEXANDER
ARCHIPENKO
*Green Concave (Woman
Combing Her Hair)*, 1913
bronze, wood base
19 ½ (height)
© Estate of Alexander
Archipenko/Artists Rights
Society (ARS), New York

BERTIL VALLIEN
Boats and Bars, ca. 1985
sandcast glass
9 ½ x 12 x 25

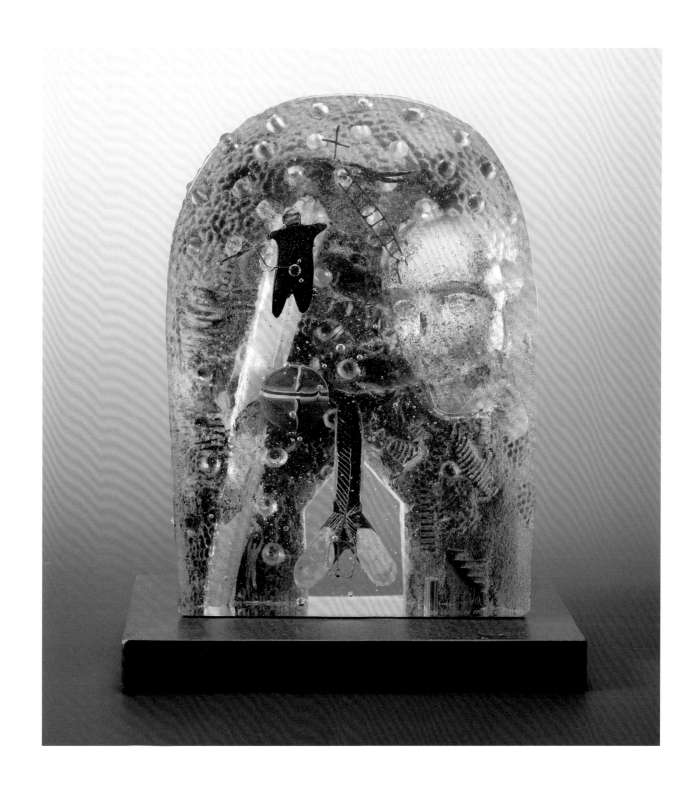

BERTIL VALLIEN
Staircase, 1991
cast glass
14 ½ x 11 ½ x 6

VIOLA FREY
Reflective Woman II,
2002
ceramic
91½ x 28 x 23

VIOLA FREY
*Pile of Things and a Man
and a Suit,* 1997–98
ceramic
27 x 25½ x 15

JOHN WILDE
Work Reconsidered #2.
A Portrait of Jesper
Dibble, 1958
oil on panel
25 x 21

SERGEI ISUPOV
To Keep in Touch, 2000
porcelain
18 x 16 ½ x 10

ROY LICHTENSTEIN
Imperfect Painting, 1988
oil and Magna on canvas
68 x 107
© Estate of Roy Lichtenstein

JIM DINE
Venusberg, 1988
painted bronze
72 x 38½ x 27
© 2004 Jim Dine/Artists
Rights Society (ARS), New York

MARVIN LIPOFSKY
*Pilchuck Summer Series
#4*, 1988–89
blown glass
13 x 14 x 14

RUDY AUTIO
Day & Night, 1988
ceramic
30 x 31 x 16

KLAUS MOJE
Untitled #27, 1992
fused glass
20 (diameter) x 3 (depth)

JUDY McKIE
Panthers (coffee table),
1996
bronze, glass
17 x 40 x 50

PATTI WARASHINA
See No Evil, 1993
ceramic
23 ½ x 14 ½ x 12 ½

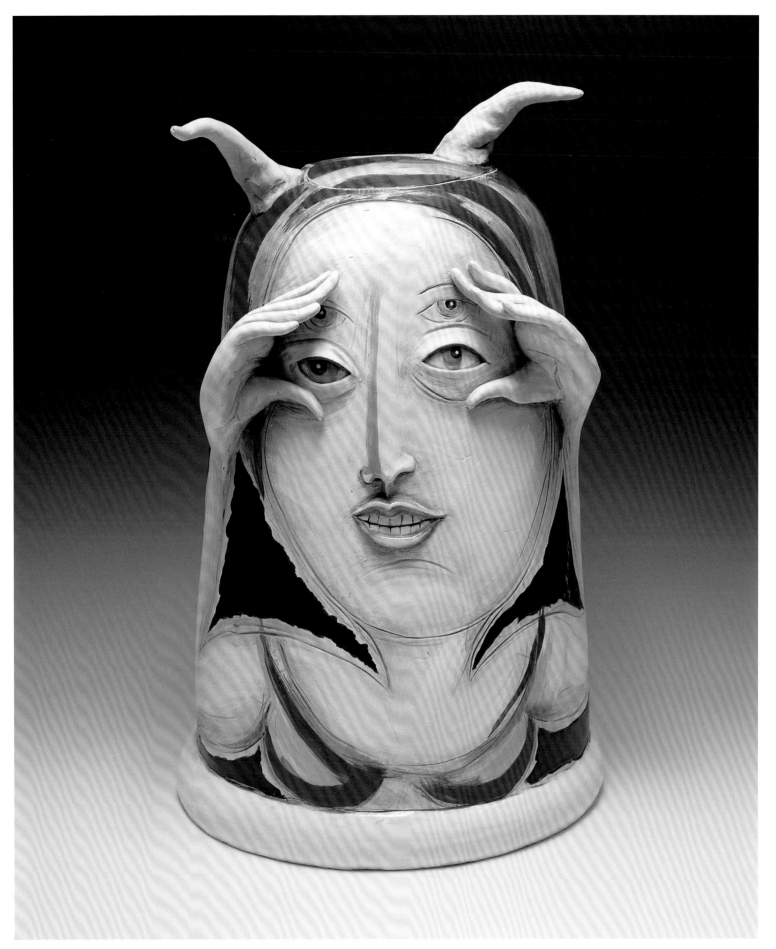

DOMINICK LABINO
Emergence, 1979
hot-worked glass
6 ¾ x 4 x 3 ½

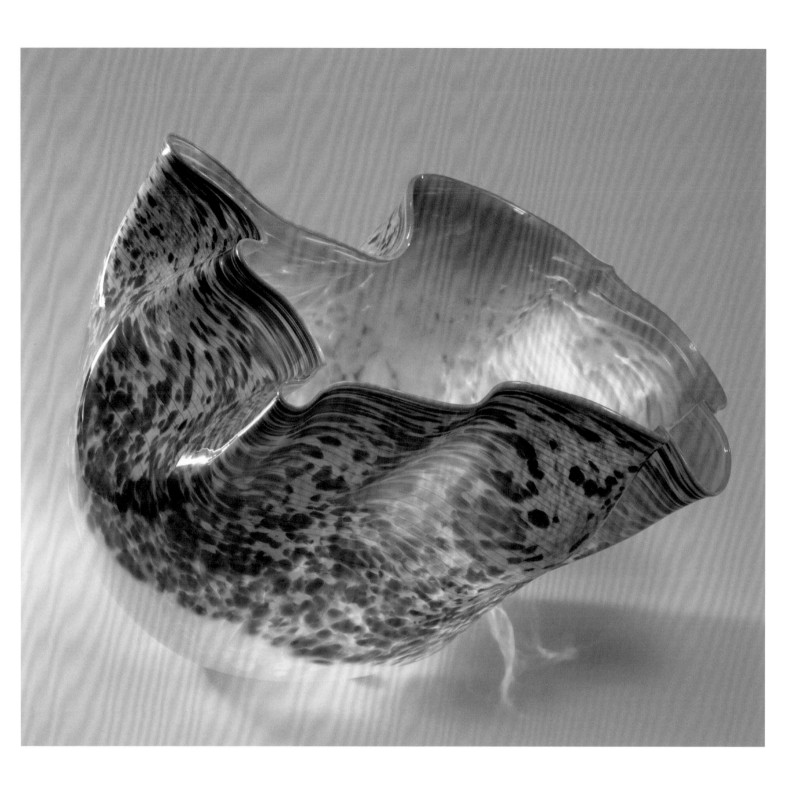

DALE CHIHULY
Macchia Basket, 1986
blown glass
18 x 20 x 24

HARVEY K.
LITTLETON
Triple Loop, 1979
hot-worked glass
14 X 15 X 12

MICHAEL GLANCY
Cloaked Ruby Sentinel,
1986
blown glass, industrial
plate glass, electro-
deposited copper
14 1/2 X 21 X 11

SUSAN
STINSMUEHLEN-
AMEND
Stained Glass Windows,
1986–87
stained glass
85½ x 28½ (6 panels);
85½ x 19½ (2 side panels
not visible in photograph)

RICHARD LINDNER
L'As de trèfle (Ace
of Clubs), 1973
oil on canvas
78 ¾ x 71
© 2004 Artists Rights Society
(ARS), New York/ADAGP Paris

JANUSZ
WALENTYNOWICZ
Yellow Twelve Pack,
2004
cast glass
9 ½ x 16 x 11

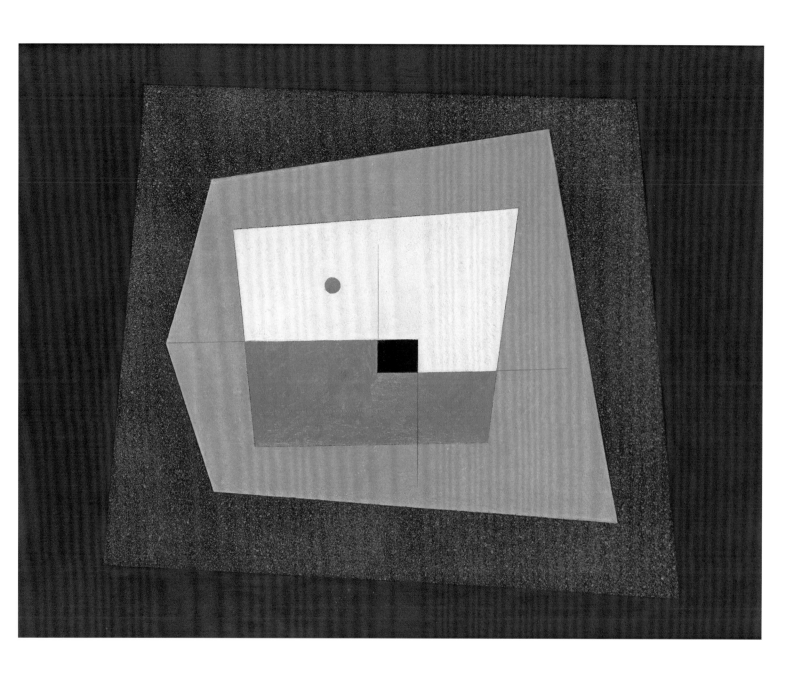

JAROSLAVA
BRYCHTOVÁ AND
STANISLAV LIBENSKÝ
The Column, 1989
cast glass
65 ¼ x 13 ¼ x 9

CHARLES GREEN
SHAW
*Abstraction with Blue,
Brown, and Gray Forms,*
1940
oil on canvasboard
14 x 18

RICK BECK
Wood Screws, 1992
cast glass
red: 13 x 5 ¾ (diameter,
head); white: 26 x 7 x 10

Sheet Metal Screws, 1992
cast glass
yellow: 7 x 4 ½ (diameter,
head); green: 7 x 4 ½
(diameter, head)

ROBERT ARNESON
Wow Too, 1990
ceramic
16 x 13 x 6 ½
Art © Estate of Robert
Arneson/Licensed by VAGA,
New York, NY

170

MARY
BAUERMEISTER
Pictionary, 1967
optical glass panels, pen
and black ink, plastic,
black-and-white photos
24 x 39 x 9½

171

JAY MUSLER
Cityscape Bowl, 1989
blown and sandblasted
glass, oil pigments
9 x 18 (diameter)

HANK MURTA ADAMS

BORN 1956 Philadelphia, Pennsylvania

EDUCATION BFA, Rhode Island School of Design, Providence, Rhode Island

Lives and works in Troy, New York; Philadelphia, Pennsylvania; and Millville, New Jersey

SELECTED PUBLIC COLLECTIONS

Birmingham Museum of Art, Birmingham, Alabama

The Contemporary Museum, Honolulu, Hawaii

Corning Museum of Glass, Corning, New York

The Detroit Institute of Arts, Detroit, Michigan

Glasmuseum, Frauenau, Germany

Glasmuseum Hentrich, Museum Kunst Palast, Düsseldorf, Germany

Hokkaido Museum of Modern Art, Sapporo, Japan

Lowe Art Museum, University of Miami, Miami, Florida

The Mint Museum of Craft + Design, Charlotte, North Carolina

mudac–Musée de design et d'arts appliqués contemporains, Lausanne, Switzerland

The Renwick Gallery of the Smithsonian American Art Museum, Smithsonian Institution, Washington, D.C.

Shimonoseki City Art Museum, Shimonoseki, Japan

Speed Art Museum, Louisville, Kentucky

Stötzle Oberglas Museum, Bärnbach, Austria

Toledo Museum of Art, Toledo, Ohio

ALEXANDER ARCHIPENKO

BORN 1880 Kiev, Ukraine

DIED 1964 New York, New York

EDUCATION Kiev Art School, Kiev, Ukraine; École des Beaux-Arts, Paris, France

SELECTED PUBLIC COLLECTIONS

The Art Institute of Chicago, Chicago, Illinois

The Cleveland Museum of Art, Cleveland, Ohio

Denver Art Museum, Denver, Colorado

The Detroit Institute of Arts, Detroit, Michigan

Musée National d'Art Moderne, Centre Georges Pompidou, Paris, France

The Museum of Modern Art, New York, New York

Neue Nationalgalerie, Berlin, Germany

Osaka Municipal Museum of Art, Osaka, Japan

Peggy Guggenheim Collection, Venice, Italy

The Rose Art Museum at Brandeis University, Waltham, Massachusetts

Seattle Art Museum, Seattle, Washington

Solomon R. Guggenheim Museum, New York, New York

Tel Aviv Museum of Art, Tel Aviv, Israel

University of Missouri–Kansas City, Kansas City, Missouri

Whitney Museum of American Art, New York, New York

ROBERT ARNESON

BORN 1930 Benicia, California

DIED 1992 Benicia, California

EDUCATION BA, California College of Arts and Crafts, Oakland, California; MFA, Mills College, Oakland, California

SELECTED PUBLIC COLLECTIONS

Aichi Prefectural Ceramic Museum, Seto City, Japan

The Art Institute of Chicago, Chicago, Illinois

Everson Museum of Art, Syracuse, New York

Hirshhorn Museum and Sculpture Garden, Smithsonian Institution,
    Washington, D.C.

Los Angeles County Museum of Art, Los Angeles, California

The Metropolitan Museum of Art, New York, New York

Mildura Arts Centre, Mildura, Victoria, Australia

Museum of Arts & Design, New York, New York

Museum of Fine Arts, Boston, Massachusetts

The Museum of Modern Art, New York, New York

The National Museum of Modern Art, Kyoto, Japan

Philadelphia Museum of Art, Philadelphia, Pennsylvania

San Francisco Museum of Modern Art, San Francisco, California

Stedelijk Museum, Amsterdam, The Netherlands

Whitney Museum of American Art, New York, New York

RUDY AUTIO

BORN 1926 Butte, Montana

EDUCATION BS, Montana State College, Bozeman, Montana; MFA,
    Washington State University, Pullman, Washington

Lives and works in Missoula, Montana

SELECTED PUBLIC COLLECTIONS

Aichi Prefectural Ceramic Art Museum, Seto City, Japan

Archie Bray Foundation for the Ceramic Arts, Helena, Montana

Designmuseo, Helsinki, Finland

Everson Museum of Art, Syracuse, New York

Millennium Collection, United States Embassy, Moscow, Russia

Museum of Arts & Design, New York, New York

Museum of Contemporary Ceramic Art, Shigaraki, Japan

Museum of Fine Arts, Boston, Massachusetts

The Nelson-Atkins Museum of Art, Kansas City, Missouri

Portland Art Museum, Portland, Oregon

The Renwick Gallery of the Smithsonian American Art Museum,
    Smithsonian Institution, Washington, D.C.

Seattle Art Museum, Seattle, Washington

Victoria and Albert Museum, London, England

World Ceramic Exposition Korea (WOCEK) Collection, Icheon World
    Ceramic Center, Icheon, Korea

Yellowstone Art Museum, Billings, Montana

MILTON AVERY

BORN 1885 Altmar, New York

DIED 1965 New York, New York

EDUCATION Hartford School, Hartford, Connecticut; Connecticut League
    of Art Students, Hartford, Connecticut

SELECTED PUBLIC COLLECTIONS

The Art Institute of Chicago, Chicago, Illinois

The Baltimore Museum of Art, Baltimore, Maryland

The Brooklyn Museum of Art, Brooklyn, New York

Hirshhorn Museum and Sculpture Garden, Smithsonian Institution,
    Washington, D.C.

Honolulu Academy of Arts, Honolulu, Hawaii

The Metropolitan Museum of Art, New York, New York

The Museum of Modern Art, New York, New York

National Gallery of Art, Washington, D.C.

The Newark Museum, Newark, New Jersey

Pennsylvania Academy of Fine Arts, Philadelphia, Pennsylvania

The Phillips Collection, Washington, D.C.

Tel Aviv Museum of Art, Tel Aviv, Israel

Wadsworth Atheneum Museum of Art, Hartford, Connecticut

Walker Art Center, Minneapolis, Minnesota

Whitney Museum of American Art, New York, New York

MARY BAUERMEISTER

BORN 1934 Frankfurt, Germany

EDUCATION self-taught

Lives and works in Cologne, Germany

SELECTED PUBLIC COLLECTIONS

Albright-Knox Art Gallery, Buffalo, New York

The Aldrich Contemporary Art Museum, Ridgefield, Connecticut

The Brooklyn Museum of Art, Brooklyn, New York

Flint Institute of Arts, Flint, Michigan

Kunstmuseum (Museum of Modern Art), Bonn, Germany

Kölnische Stadtmuseum (Cologne City Museum), Cologne, Germany

Museum Ludwig, Cologne, Germany

The Museum of Modern Art, New York, New York

Solomon R. Guggenheim Museum, New York, New York

Stedelijk Museum, Amsterdam, The Netherlands

Whitney Museum of American Art, New York, New York

RICK BECK

BORN 1960 Edmonton, Canada

EDUCATION BA, Hastings College, Hastings, Nebraska; MFA, Southern
    Illinois University, Carbondale, Illinois

Lives and works in Spruce Pine, North Carolina

SELECTED PUBLIC COLLECTIONS

Asheville Art Museum, Asheville, North Carolina

Columbia Museum of Art, Columbia, South Carolina

Glasmuseet Ebeltoft, Ebeltoft, Denmark

Hickory Museum of Art, Hickory, North Carolina

The Mint Museum of Craft + Design, Charlotte, North Carolina

North Carolina State University, Raleigh, North Carolina

Racine Art Museum, Racine, Wisconsin

HOWARD BEN TRÉ

BORN 1949 Brooklyn, New York

EDUCATION BSA, Portland State University, Portland, Oregon; MFA,
    Rhode Island School of Design, Providence, Rhode Island

Lives and works in Providence, Rhode Island

SELECTED PUBLIC COLLECTIONS

Centro Cultural / Arte Contemporaneo, Mexico City, Mexico

The Detroit Institute of Arts, Detroit, Michigan
de Young Museum, San Francisco, California
Hirshhorn Museum and Sculpture Garden, Smithsonian Institution,
    Washington, D.C.
Hokkaido Museum of Modern Art, Sapporo, Japan
Los Angeles County Museum of Art, Los Angeles, California
The Metropolitan Museum of Art, New York, New York
Musée d'Art Moderne et d'Art Contemporain, Nice, France
Museum of Arts & Design, New York, New York
Museum of Fine Arts, Boston, Massachusetts
The Museum of Fine Arts, Houston, Texas
National Museum of Modern Art, Tokyo, Japan
Philadelphia Museum of Art, Philadelphia, Pennsylvania
Seattle Art Museum, Seattle, Washington
Toledo Museum of Art, Toledo, Ohio

ILYA BOLOTOWSKY

BORN 1907 Petrograd, Russia
DIED 1981 New York, New York
EDUCATION National Academy of Design, New York, New York
SELECTED PUBLIC COLLECTIONS
Academy of Fine Arts, Calcutta, India
The Art Institute of Chicago, Chicago, Illinois
The Brooklyn Museum of Art, Brooklyn, New York
    Carnegie Museum of Art, Pittsburgh, Pennsylvania
Göteborg Kunstmuseum (Göteborg Museum of Art), Göteborg, Sweden
Hirshhorn Museum and Sculpture Garden, Smithsonian Institution,
    Washington, D.C.
The Israel Museum, Jerusalem, Israel
The Metropolitan Museum of Art, New York, New York
Musée d'Art Moderne, Céret, France
Museum of Fine Arts, Boston, Massachusetts
The Museum of Modern Art, New York, New York
Philadelphia Museum of Art, Philadelphia, Pennsylvania
San Francisco Museum of Modern Art, San Francisco, California
Walker Art Center, Minneapolis, Minnesota
Whitney Museum of American Art, New York, New York

JAROSLAVA BRYCHTOVÁ

BORN 1924 Železný Brod, Czechoslovakia
EDUCATION Academy of Applied Arts, Prague, Czechoslovakia
Lives and works in Železný Brod, Czech Republic
SELECTED PUBLIC COLLECTIONS (in collaboration with Stanislav Libenský)
Corning Museum of Glass, Corning, New York
Design Museum, Ghent, Belgium
Los Angeles County Museum of Art, Los Angeles, California
The Metropolitan Museum of Art, New York, New York
The Mint Museum of Craft + Design, Charlotte, North Carolina
mudac–Musée de design et d'arts appliqués contemporains,
    Lausanne, Switzerland
Musée des Arts Décoratifs, Paris, France
El Museo de Bellas Artes de Valencia, Valencia, Spain

Museum of Applied Arts and Sciences, Sydney, Australia
Museum of Art, Moscow, Russia
Narodni Galerie (National Gallery), Prague, Czech Republic
National Museum of Modern Art, Tokyo, Japan
Rijksmuseum, Amsterdam, The Netherlands
Toledo Museum of Art, Toledo, Ohio
Victoria and Albert Museum, London, England

LUCIO BUBACCO

BORN 1957 Murano (Venice), Italy
EDUCATION informal apprenticeships with father (an internationally
    famous glass artist) and other Murano glass artists; self-taught
    in flameworking; studied drawing and painting anatomy with
    Alessandro Rossi
Lives and works in Murano, Italy
SELECTED PUBLIC COLLECTIONS
Corning Museum of Glass, Corning, New York
J. & L. Lobmeyr Collection, Vienna, Austria
Kitaichi Venetian Art Museum, Otaru, Japan
Museo del Vidrio (Glass Museum), Monterrey, Mexico
Museo Vetrario (Glass Museum), Murano, Italy
Museum Boijmans Van Beuningen, Rotterdam, The Netherlands
Museum of American Glass, Wheaton Village, Millville, New Jersey
Museum of Arts & Design, New York, New York
National Liberty Museum, Philadelphia, Pennsylvania
Niijima Contemporary Glass Art Museum, Niijima, Japan
Tampa Museum of Art, Tampa, Florida

ALEXANDER CALDER

BORN 1898 Lawton, Pennsylvania
DIED 1976 New York, New York
EDUCATION Stevens Institute of Technology, Hoboken, New Jersey;
    Art Students League, New York, New York
SELECTED PUBLIC COLLECTIONS
de Young Museum, San Francisco, California
The Metropolitan Museum of Art, New York, New York
Musée de Grenoble, Grenoble, France
Musées royaux des Beaux-Arts de Belgique (Royal Museums of Fine
    Arts of Belgium), Brussels, Belgium
Museo Nacional Centro de Arte Reina Sofía, Madrid, Spain
Museu de Arte de São Paulo, São Paulo, Brazil
The Museum of Fine Arts, Houston, Texas
National Gallery of Art, Washington, D.C.
National Gallery of Australia, Canberra, Australia
Peggy Guggenheim Collection, Venice, Italy
The Renwick Gallery of the Smithsonian American Art Museum,
    Smithsonian Institution, Washington, D.C.
San Francisco Museum of Modern Art, San Francisco, California
Städelmuseum, Frankfurt, Germany
Tate Gallery, London, England
Tehran Museum of Contemporary Art, Tehran, Iran

WILLIAM CARLSON

BORN 1950 Dover, Ohio

EDUCATION BFA, Cleveland Institute of Art, Cleveland, Ohio; MFA, Alfred
  University, New York State College of Ceramics, Alfred, New York;
  Pilchuck Glass School, Stanwood, Washington; Art Students League,
  New York, New York

Lives and works in Coral Gables, Florida

SELECTED PUBLIC COLLECTIONS

Corning Museum of Glass, Corning, New York

The Detroit Institute of Arts, Detroit, Michigan

The Evansville Museum of Arts, History and Science, Evansville, Indiana

Hokkaido Museum of Modern Art, Sapporo, Japan

Huntington Museum of Art, Huntington, West Virginia

Krannert Art Museum, Champaign, Illinois

Hunter Museum of American Art, Chattanooga, Tennessee

Indianapolis Museum of Art, Indianapolis, Indiana

Los Angeles County Museum of Art, Los Angeles, California

The Metropolitan Museum of Art, New York, New York

Milwaukee Art Museum, Milwaukee, Wisconsin

The Mint Museum of Craft + Design, Charlotte, North Carolina

mudac-Musée de design et d'arts appliqués contemporains,
  Lausanne, Switzerland

The National Museum of Modern Art, Kyoto, Japan

The Saint Louis Art Museum, St. Louis, Missouri

SIR ANTHONY CARO

BORN 1924 New Malden, England

EDUCATION Christ's College, Cambridge, England; Regent Street
  Polytechnic, Royal Academy Schools, London, England

Lives and works in London, England

SELECTED PUBLIC COLLECTIONS

Fondation Veranneman, Kruishoutem, Belgium

Hirshhorn Museum and Sculpture Garden, Smithsonian Institution,
  Washington, D.C.

The Israel Museum, Jerusalem, Israel

Johannesburg Art Gallery, Johannesburg, South Africa

Kunsthalle Würth, Schwäbisch Hall, Germany

Los Angeles County Museum of Art, Los Angeles, California

The Metropolitan Museum of Art, New York, New York

Musée National d'Art Moderne, Centre Georges Pompidou,
  Paris, France

Museo de Arte Contemporaneo de Caracas Sofía Imber,
  Caracas, Venezuela

Museum of Contemporary Art, Tokyo, Japan

Museum of Fine Arts, Boston, Massachusetts

The Museum of Modern Art, New York, New York

Philadelphia Museum of Art, Philadelphia, Pennsylvania

Tate Gallery, London, England

Queensland Art Gallery, Brisbane, Australia

SYDNEY CASH

BORN 1941 Detroit, Michigan

EDUCATION Wayne State University, Detroit, Michigan; L'Alliance
  Française, Paris, France

Lives and works in Marlboro, New York

SELECTED PUBLIC COLLECTIONS

Ball State University Museum of Art, Muncie, Indiana

Corning Museum of Glass, Corning, New York

The Detroit Institute of Arts, Detroit, Michigan

Lowe Art Museum, University of Miami, Miami, Florida

mudac-Musée de design et d'arts appliqués contemporains,
  Lausanne, Switzerland

Musée des Arts Décoratifs, Paris, France

The Museum of Fine Arts, Houston, Houston, Texas

The Museum of Modern Art, New York, New York

The Nelson A. Rockefeller Collection, Morristown, New Jersey

The Renwick Gallery of the Smithsonian American Art Museum,
  Smithsonian Institution, Washington, D.C.

SANDRO CHIA

BORN 1946 Florence, Italy

EDUCATION Accademia di Belle Arti, Florence, Italy

Lives and works in New York, New York, and Montalcino, Siena, Italy

SELECTED PUBLIC COLLECTIONS

Groninger Museum, Groningen, The Netherlands

Hirshhorn Museum and Sculpture Garden, Smithsonian Institution,
  Washington, D.C.

Musée National d'Art Moderne, Centre Georges Pompidou, Paris, France

The Museum of Modern Art, New York, New York

National Gallery of Scotland, Edinburgh, Scotland

Solomon R. Guggenheim Museum, New York, New York

Städtisches Museum (Municipal Museum), Mönchengladbach, Germany

Stedelijk Museum, Amsterdam, The Netherlands

Tate Gallery, London, England

DALE CHIHULY

BORN 1941 Tacoma, Washington

EDUCATION BA, University of Washington, Seattle, Washington; MS,
  University of Wisconsin–Madison, Madison, Wisconsin; MFA Rhode
  Island School of Design, Providence, Rhode Island

Lives and works in Seattle, Washington

SELECTED PUBLIC COLLECTIONS

Corning Museum of Glass, Corning, New York

Glasmuseet Ebeltoft, Ebeltoft, Denmark

The Israel Museum, Jerusalem, Israel

Los Angeles County Museum of Art, Los Angeles, California

The Metropolitan Museum of Art, New York, New York

mudac-Musée de design et d'arts appliqués contemporains,
  Lausanne, Switzerland

Musée des Arts Décoratifs, Paris, France

Museo del Vidrio (Glass Museum), Monterrey, Mexico

Museo Vetrario (Glass Museum), Murano, Italy

Museum of Arts & Design, New York, New York
National Gallery of Australia, Canberra, Australia
National Museum of Modern Art, Tokyo, Japan
Nationalmuseum, Stockholm, Sweden
The Renwick Gallery of the Smithsonian American Art Museum,
    Smithsonian Institution, Washington, D.C.
Victoria and Albert Museum, London, England

DANIEL CLAYMAN

BORN 1957 Lynn, Massachusetts
EDUCATION BFA, Rhode Island School of Design, Providence, Rhode
    Island; University of Massachusetts, Amherst, Massachusetts;
    Connecticut College, New London, Connecticut
Lives and works in Rumford, Rhode Island
SELECTED PUBLIC COLLECTIONS
The Cleveland Museum of Art, Cleveland, Ohio
Corning Museum of Glass, Corning, New York
de Young Museum, San Francisco, California
Fukui City Museum of Art, Fukui, Japan
Milwaukee Art Museum, Milwaukee, Wisconsin
Museum of American Glass, Wheaton Village, Millville, New Jersey
Museum of Art, Rhode Island School of Design, Providence, Rhode Island
Museum of Arts & Design, New York, New York
Pilchuck Glass School, Stanwood, Washington
Portland Museum of Art, Portland, Maine
Racine Art Museum, Racine, Wisconsin
The Renwick Gallery of the Smithsonian American Art Museum,
    Smithsonian Institution, Washington, D.C.
Toledo Museum of Art, Toledo, Ohio

DAN DAILEY

BORN 1947 Philadelphia, Pennsylvania
EDUCATION BFA, Philadelphia College of Art, Philadelphia, Pennsylvania;
    MFA, Rhode Island School of Design, Providence, Rhode Island
Lives and works in Kensington, New Hampshire
SELECTED PUBLIC COLLECTIONS
Corning Museum of Glass, Corning, New York
The Detroit Institute of Arts, Detroit, Michigan
High Museum of Art, Atlanta, Georgia
Kestner Museum, Hanover, Germany
Los Angeles County Museum of Art, Los Angeles, California
Milwaukee Art Museum, Milwaukee, Wisconsin
mudac–Musée de design et d'arts appliqués contemporains,
    Lausanne, Switzerland
Musée des Arts Décoratifs, Paris, France
Museum of Arts & Design, New York, New York
Museum of Fine Arts, Boston, Massachusetts
National Gallery of Victoria, Melbourne, Australia
The National Museum of Modern Art, Kyoto, Japan
Philadelphia Museum of Art, Philadelphia, Pennsylvania

The Renwick Gallery of the Smithsonian American Art Museum;
    Smithsonian Institution, Washington, D.C.
Royal Ontario Museum, Toronto, Canada

OLGA DE AMARAL

BORN 1932 Bogotá, Colombia
EDUCATION University of Cundinamarca, Bogotá, Colombia;
    Cranbrook Academy of Art, Bloomfield Hills, Michigan
Lives and works in Bogotá, Colombia
SELECTED PUBLIC COLLECTIONS
The Art Institute of Chicago, Chicago, Illinois
The Cleveland Museum of Art, Cleveland, Ohio
de Young Museum, San Francisco, California
Denver Art Museum, Denver, Colorado
The Metropolitan Museum of Art, New York, New York
Musée d'Art Moderne de la Ville de Paris, Paris, France
Musée Jean Luçat et de la Tapisserie Contemporaine, Angers, France
Museo de Arte Moderno, Bogotá, Colombia
Museo del Instituto de Arte Contemporáneo, Lima, Peru
Museum Bellerive, Zurich, Switzerland
Museum of Arts & Design, New York, New York
The Museum of Modern Art, New York, New York
The National Museum of Modern Art, Kyoto, Japan
The Renwick Gallery of the Smithsonian American Art Museum,
    Smithsonian Institution, Washington, D.C.
Toledo Museum of Art, Toledo, Ohio

BURGOYNE DILLER

BORN 1906 New York, New York
DIED 1965 Brooklyn, New York
EDUCATION Michigan State University, Lansing, Michigan; Art
    Students League (under Hans Hofmann and George Grosz),
    New York, New York
SELECTED PUBLIC COLLECTIONS
The Art Institute of Chicago, Chicago, Illinois
Corcoran Gallery of Art, Washington, D.C.
Elvehjem Museum of Art, University of Wisconsin–Madison,
    Madison, Wisconsin
Gemeentemuseum, The Hague, The Netherlands
Hirshhorn Museum and Sculpture Garden, Smithsonian Institution,
    Washington, D.C.
The Metropolitan Museum of Art, New York, New York
The Museum of Fine Arts, Houston, Texas
The Museum of Modern Art, New York, New York
National Gallery of Art, Washington, D.C.
The Renwick Gallery of the Smithsonian American Art Museum,
    Smithsonian Institution, Washington, D.C.
San Francisco Museum of Modern Art, San Francisco, California
Solomon R. Guggenheim Museum, New York, New York
Walker Art Center, Minneapolis, Minnesota

Whitney Museum of American Art, New York, New York
Yale University Art Gallery, New Haven, Connecticut

JIM DINE

BORN 1935 Cincinnati, Ohio
EDUCATION University of Cincinnati, Cincinnati, Ohio; Boston Museum
    School, Boston, Massachusetts; BFA, Ohio University, Athens, Ohio
Lives and works in New York, New York
SELECTED PUBLIC COLLECTIONS
The Art Institute of Chicago, Chicago, Illinois
The Hakone Open-Air Museum, Hakone-machi, Japan
Hirshhorn Museum and Sculpture Garden, Smithsonian Institution,
    Washington, D.C.
The Israel Museum, Jerusalem, Israel
The Metropolitan Museum of Art, New York, New York
Moderna Museet, Stockholm, Sweden
Musée National d'Art Moderne, Centre Georges Pompidou, Paris, France
Museum of Fine Arts, Boston, Massachusetts
The Museum of Modern Art, New York, New York
National Gallery of Art, Washington, D.C.
San Francisco Museum of Modern Art, San Francisco, California
Solomon R. Guggenheim Museum, New York, New York
Stedelijk Museum, Amsterdam, The Netherlands
Tate Gallery, London, England
Whitney Museum of American Art, New York, New York

JEAN DUBUFFET

BORN 1901 Le Havre, France
DIED 1985 Paris, France
EDUCATION Académie Julian, Paris, France; self-taught
SELECTED PUBLIC COLLECTIONS
de Young Museum, San Francisco, California
Hirshhorn Museum and Sculpture Garden, Smithsonian Institution,
    Washington D.C.
Kunstmuseum Basel, Basel, Switzerland
The Metropolitan Museum of Art, New York, New York
mumok—Museum Moderner Kunst, Stiftung Ludwig (Museum
    of Modern Art, Ludwig Foundation), Vienna, Austria
Museo Nacional Centro de Arte Reina Sofía, Madrid, Spain
Museo Nacional de Bellas Artes, Buenos Aires, Argentina
Museu d'Art Contemporani de Barcelona, Barcelona, Spain
Museum of Fine Arts, Boston, Massachusetts
The Museum of Modern Art, New York, New York
National Gallery of Art, Washington, D.C.
National Gallery of Australia, Canberra, Australia
Staatsgalerie Stuttgart, Stuttgart, Germany
Städelmuseum, Frankfurt, Germany
Tate Gallery, London, England

ERWIN EISCH

BORN 1927 Frauenau, Germany
EDUCATION apprenticeship in glass engraving workshop of father,
    Valentin Eisch; Academy of Fine Arts, Munich, Germany
Lives and works in Frauenau, Germany
SELECTED PUBLIC COLLECTIONS
Bayerisches Nationalmuseum (Bavarian National Museum),
    Munich, Germany
Corning Museum of Glass, Corning, New York
Elvehjem Museum of Art, University of Wisconsin–Madison,
    Madison, Wisconsin
Glasmuseet Ebeltoft, Ebeltoft, Denmark
Kunstgewerbemuseum (Museum of Applied Arts), Berlin, Germany
Leigh Yawkey Woodson Art Museum, Wausau, Wisconsin
MAK—Museum für Angewandte Kunst (Museum of Applied Arts),
    Vienna, Austria
Musée des Arts Décoratifs, Paris, France
Museum Bellerive, Zurich, Switzerland
Museum Boijmans Van Beuningen, Rotterdam, The Netherlands
Museum für Angewandte Kunst (Museum of Applied Arts),
    Frankfurt, Germany
Museum of Art, Yokohama, Japan
The National Museum of Modern Art, Kyoto, Japan
Smithsonian Institution, Washington, D.C.
Toledo Museum of Art, Toledo, Ohio

VIOLA FREY

BORN 1933 Lodi, California
DIED 2004 Oakland, California
EDUCATION BFA, California College of Arts and Crafts, Oakland,
    California; MFA, Tulane University, New Orleans, Louisiana
SELECTED PUBLIC COLLECTIONS
The Contemporary Museum, Honolulu, Hawaii
The Detroit Institute of Arts, Detroit, Michigan
Everson Museum of Art, Syracuse, New York
Los Angeles County Museum of Art, Los Angeles, California
The Metropolitan Museum of Art, New York, New York
The Minneapolis Institute of Arts, Minneapolis, Minnesota
Musée de Céramique, Sèvres, France
Museum of Arts & Design, New York, New York
Museum of Arts and Sciences, Macon, Georgia
The Museum of Contemporary Art, Los Angeles, California
Museum of Contemporary Ceramic Art, Shigaraki, Japan
Oakland Museum of California, Oakland, California
Philadelphia Museum of Art, Philadelphia, Pennsylvania
San Francisco Museum of Modern Art, San Francisco, California
Whitney Museum of American Art, New York, New York

KYOHEI FUJITA

BORN 1920 Tokyo, Japan
DIED 2004 Tokyo, Japan
EDUCATION Tokyo Academy of Arts, Tokyo, Japan

SELECTED PUBLIC COLLECTIONS

The Art Gallery of Western Australia, Perth, Australia

Corning Museum of Glass, Corning, New York

Glasmuseet Ebeltoft, Ebeltoft, Denmark

Glasmuseum, Frauenau, Germany

Göteborg Kunstmuseum (Göteborg Museum of Art), Göteborg, Sweden

Hokkaido Museum of Modern Art, Sapporo, Japan

Kunstindustrimuseet (Museum of Decorative Arts), Copenhagen, Denmark

Leigh Yawkey Woodson Art Museum, Wausau, Wisconsin

Musée des Arts Décoratifs, Paris, France

Museum of Art, Yokohama, Japan

mudac–Musée de design et d'arts appliqués contemporains, Lausanne, Switzerland

Museum of Arts & Design, New York, New York

National Museum of Modern Art, Tokyo, Japan

Toledo Museum of Art, Toledo, Ohio

Victoria and Albert Museum, London, England

ED GARMAN

BORN 1914 Detroit, Michigan

DIED 2004 Imperial Beach, California

EDUCATION University of New Mexico, Albuquerque, New Mexico

SELECTED PUBLIC COLLECTIONS

Addison Gallery of American Art, Andover, Massachusetts

Henry Art Gallery, University of Washington, Seattle, Washington

Jonson Gallery of the University of New Mexico Art Museum, Albuquerque, New Mexico

Portland Art Museum, Portland, Oregon

Roswell Museum and Art Center, Roswell, New Mexico

The Renwick Gallery of the Smithsonian American Art Museum, Smithsonian Institution, Washington, D.C.

Sheldon Memorial Art Gallery, University of Nebraska, Lincoln, Nebraska

MICHAEL GLANCY

BORN 1950 Detroit, Michigan

EDUCATION BFA, University of Denver, Colorado; BFA, MFA, Rhode Island School of Design, Providence, Rhode Island

Lives and works in Rehoboth, Massachusetts

SELECTED PUBLIC COLLECTIONS

The Art Gallery of Western Australia, Perth, Australia

Corning Museum of Glass, Corning, New York

The Detroit Institute of Arts, Detroit, Michigan

Essener Glasgalerie, Essen, Germany

Glasmuseet Ebeltoft, Ebeltoft, Denmark

Hokkaido Museum of Modern Art, Sapporo, Japan

Los Angeles County Museum of Art, Los Angeles, California

The Metropolitan Museum of Art, New York, New York

Musée de design et d'arts appliqués contemporains, Lausanne, Switzerland

Musée des Arts Décoratifs, Paris, France

Museum of Arts & Design, New York, New York

Philadelphia Museum of Art, Philadelphia, Pennsylvania

The Renwick Gallery of the Smithsonian American Art Museum, Smithsonian Institution, Washington, D.C.

Toledo Museum of Art, Toledo, Ohio

Victoria and Albert Museum, London, England

GEORGE GROSZ

BORN 1910 Berlin, Germany

DIED 1959 Berlin, Germany

EDUCATION Dresden Academy of Art, Dresden, Germany; School of Applied Arts, Berlin, Germany; Royal Academy of Art, Dresden, Germany; College of Arts and Crafts, Berlin, Germany

SELECTED PUBLIC COLLECTIONS

The Brooklyn Museum of Art, Brooklyn, New York

de Young Museum, San Francisco, California

Dallas Museum of Art, Dallas, Texas

Denver Art Museum, Denver, Colorado

High Museum of Art, Atlanta, Georgia

Hirshhorn Museum and Sculpture Garden, Smithsonian Institution, Washington, D.C.

The Metropolitan Museum of Art, New York, New York

The Museum of Modern Art, New York, New York

Neue Nationalgalerie, Berlin, Germany

The Newark Museum, Newark, New Jersey

Phoenix Art Museum, Phoenix, Arizona

The Renwick Gallery of the Smithsonian American Art Museum, Smithsonian Institution, Washington, D.C.

Tate Gallery, London, England

Wadsworth Atheneum Museum of Art, Hartford, Connecticut

Whitney Museum of American Art, New York, New York

AL HELD

BORN 1928 Brooklyn, New York

EDUCATION Art Students League, New York, New York; Académie de la Grande Chaumière, Paris, France

Lives and works in Woodstock, New York

SELECTED PUBLIC COLLECTIONS

Delaware Art Museum, Wilmington, Delaware

Fogg Art Museum, Harvard University Art Museums, Cambridge, Massachusetts

Hirshhorn Museum and Sculpture Garden, Smithsonian Institution, Washington, D.C.

Kunsthaus Zürich, Zürich, Switzerland

The Metropolitan Museum of Art, New York, New York

The Museum of Modern Art, New York, New York

San Francisco Museum of Modern Art, San Francisco, California

Staatsgalerie Stuttgart, Stuttgart, Germany

Whitney Museum of American Art, New York, New York

Yale University Art Gallery, New Haven, Connecticut

DAVID HOCKNEY

BORN 1937 Bradford, England
EDUCATION Royal College of Art, London, England
Lives and works near Los Angeles, California

SELECTED PUBLIC COLLECTIONS

The Art Institute of Chicago, Chicago, Illinois
The Detroit Institute of Arts, Detroit, Michigan
J. Paul Getty Museum, Los Angeles, California
Kunstmuseum Basel, Basel, Switzerland
mumok—Museum Moderner Kunst, Stiftung Ludwig, Wien (Museum
    of Modern Art, Ludwig Foundation), Vienna, Austria
The Metropolitan Museum of Art, New York, New York
Musée National d'Art Moderne, Centre Georges Pompidou, Paris, France
Museum Ludwig, Cologne, Germany
Museum of Contemporary Art, Tokyo, Japan
Museum of Fine Arts, Boston, Massachusetts
The Museum of Modern Art, New York, New York
Olinda Museum, São Paulo, Brazil
Stedelijk Museum, Amsterdam, The Netherlands
Tate Gallery, London, England
The Renwick Gallery of the Smithsonian American Art Museum,
    Smithsonian Institution, Washington, D.C.

HANS HOFMANN

BORN 1880 Weissburg, Germany
DIED 1966 New York, New York
EDUCATION Moriz Heyman's art school in Munich, Germany; Académie
    de la Grand Chaumière and Académie Colarossi, Paris, France

SELECTED PUBLIC COLLECTIONS

The Art Institute of Chicago, Chicago, Illinois
Germanische Nationalmuseum, Nürnberg, Germany
Hirshhorn Museum and Sculpture Garden, Smithsonian Institution,
    Washington, D.C.
Los Angeles County Museum of Art, Los Angeles, California
The Metropolitan Museum of Art, New York, New York
Montreal Museum of Fine Arts, Montreal, Canada
Musée de Grenoble, Grenoble, France
Museu d'Art Contemporani de Barcelona, Barcelona, Spain
Museum of Fine Arts, Boston, Massachusetts
The Museum of Modern Art, New York, New York
National Gallery of Art, Washington, D.C.
National Gallery of Australia, Canberra, Australia
Philadelphia Museum of Art, Philadelphia, Pennsylvania
Tate Gallery, London, England
Whitney Museum of American Art, New York, New York

SERGEI ISUPOV

BORN 1963 Stavrapole, Russia, Soviet Union
EDUCATION BA, MFA, Art Institute, Tallinn, Estonia, Soviet Union;
    Ukrainian State Art School, Kiev, Ukraine, Soviet Union
Lives and works in Richmond, Virginia

SELECTED PUBLIC COLLECTIONS

Arkansas Arts Center, Little Rock, Arkansas
Carnegie Museum of Art, Pittsburgh, Pennsylvania
Everson Museum of Art, Syracuse, New York
Kunstindustrimuseet (Museum of Applied Art), Oslo, Norway
Los Angeles County Museum of Art, Los Angeles, California
The Mint Museum of Craft + Design, Charlotte, North Carolina
Museum of Applied Art, Tumen, Russia
Museum of Contemporary Ceramics, Kecskemet, Hungary
Nordenfjeldske Kunstindustrimuseum (Norwegian Museum of Decorative
    Arts), Trondheim
Racine Art Museum, Racine, Wisconsin
Tarbekunst (Museum of Applied Art), Tallinn, Estonia

JOEY KIRKPATRICK

BORN 1952 Des Moines, Iowa
EDUCATION BFA, University of Iowa, Iowa City, Iowa; Iowa State University,
    Ames, Iowa; Pilchuck Glass School, Stanwood, Washington
Lives and works in Seattle, Washington

SELECTED PUBLIC COLLECTIONS (collaborative work with Flora Mace)

Broadfield House Glass Museum, West Midlands, England
Corning Museum of Glass, Corning, New York
The Detroit Institute of Arts, Detroit, Michigan
Glasmuseet Ebeltoft, Ebeltoft, Denmark
Hokkaido Museum of Modern Art, Sapporo, Japan
Kitazawa Glass Museum, Lake Suwa, Japan
Leigh Yawkey Woodson Art Museum, Wausau, Wisconsin
The Metropolitan Museum of Art, New York, New York
mudac–Musée de design et d'arts appliqués contemporains,
    Lausanne, Switzerland
Racine Art Museum, Racine, Wisconsin
The Renwick Gallery of the Smithsonian American Art Museum,
    Smithsonian Institution, Washington, D.C.
Seattle Art Museum, Seattle, Washington
Speed Art Museum, Louisville, Kentucky
Tacoma Art Museum, Tacoma, Washington
Toledo Museum of Art, Toledo, Ohio

SILAS KOPF

BORN 1949 Warren, Pennsylvania
EDUCATION Princeton University, Princeton, New Jersey; apprenticeship
    with Wendell Castle; École Boulle, Paris, France
Lives and works in Northampton, Massachusetts

SELECTED PUBLIC COLLECTIONS

Museum of Arts & Design, New York, New York
The Museum of Fine Arts, Springfield, Massachusetts
Smith College Museum of Art, Northampton, Massachusetts
Yale University Art Gallery, New Haven, Connecticut

JON KUHN

BORN 1949 Chicago, Illinois

EDUCATION BFA, Washburn University, Topeka, Kansas; MFA, Virginia Commonwealth University, Richmond, Virginia

Lives and works in Winston-Salem, North Carolina

SELECTED PUBLIC COLLECTIONS

Carnegie Museum of Art, Pittsburgh, Pennsylvania

Chrysler Museum of Art, Norfolk, Virginia

Corning Museum of Glass, Corning, New York

The Detroit Institute of Arts, Detroit, Michigan

Glasmuseet Ebeltoft, Ebeltoft, Denmark

Hsinchu Municipal Glass Museum, Hsinchu, Taiwan

The Metropolitan Museum of Art, New York, New York

Milwaukee Art Museum, Milwaukee, Wisconsin

The Mint Museum of Craft + Design, Charlotte, North Carolina

mudac–Musée de design et d'arts appliqués contemporains, Lausanne, Switzerland

Museo del Vidrio (Glass Museum), Monterrey, Mexico

Museum für Kunst und Gewerbe (Museum of Art and Industry), Hamburg, Germany

Museum of American Glass, Wheaton Village, Millville, New Jersey

The Renwick Gallery of the Smithsonian American Art Museum, Smithsonian Institution, Washington, D.C.

Royal Ontario Museum, Toronto, Canada

DOMINICK LABINO

BORN 1910 Fairmont City, Pennsylvania

DIED 1987 Grand Rapids, Ohio

EDUCATION Carnegie Institute of Technology, Pittsburgh, Pennsylvania; Toledo Museum School of Design, Toledo, Ohio

SELECTED PUBLIC COLLECTIONS

The Art Institute of Chicago, Chicago, Illinois

The Cleveland Museum of Art, Cleveland, Ohio

Corning Museum of Glass, Corning, New York

The Detroit Institute of the Arts, Detroit, Michigan

Kunstgewerbemuseum (Museum of Applied Arts), Berlin, Germany

The Metropolitan Museum of Art, New York, New York

Pilkington Glass Museum, St. Helens, England

The Renwick Gallery of the Smithsonian American Art Museum, Smithsonian Institution, Washington, D.C.

Smithsonian Institution, Washington, D.C.

Toledo Museum of Art, Toledo, Ohio

Victoria and Albert Museum, London, England

STANSILAV LIBENSKÝ

BORN 1921 Sezemice, Czechoslovakia

DIED 2002 Železný Brod, Czech Republic

EDUCATION Academy of Applied Arts, Prague, Czechoslovakia

SELECTED PUBLIC COLLECTIONS (in collaboration with Jaroslava Brychtová)

Corning Museum of Glass, Corning, New York

Design Museum, Ghent, Belgium

Glasmuseum Hentrich, Museum Kunst Palast, Düsseldorf, Germany

Los Angeles County Museum of Art, Los Angeles, California

mudac–Musée de design et d'arts appliqués contemporains, Lausanne, Switzerland

The Metropolitan Museum of Art, New York, New York

Musée des Arts Décoratifs, Paris, France

Muzeum Narodowe (National Museum), Wroclaw, Poland

Museum of Applied Arts and Sciences, Sydney, Australia

Museum of Art, Moscow, Russia

Narodni Galerie (National Gallery), Prague, Czech Republic

National Museum of Modern Art, Tokyo, Japan

Rijksmuseum, Amsterdam, The Netherlands

Toledo Museum of Art, Toledo, Ohio

Victoria and Albert Museum, London, England

ROY LICHTENSTEIN

BORN 1923 New York, New York

DIED 1997 Southampton, New York

EDUCATION BFA, MFA, School of Fine Arts at Ohio State University, Columbus, Ohio

SELECTED PUBLIC COLLECTIONS

20er Haus (Museum of the 20th Century), Vienna, Austria

The Art Institute of Chicago, Chicago, Illinois

Dallas Museum of Art, Dallas, Texas

The Detroit Institute of the Arts, Detroit, Michigan

The Metropolitan Museum of Art, New York, New York

The Minneapolis Institute of Arts, Minneapolis, Minnesota

Moderna Museet, Stockholm, Sweden

National Gallery of Art, Washington, D.C.

The Newark Museum, Newark, New Jersey

The Renwick Gallery of the Smithsonian American Art Museum, Smithsonian Institution, Washington, D.C.

San Francisco Museum of Modern Art, San Francisco, California

Stedelijk Museum, Amsterdam, The Netherlands

Tate Gallery, London, England

Wallraf-Richartz-Museum–Fondation Corboud, Cologne, Germany

Whitney Museum of American Art, New York, New York

RICHARD LINDNER

BORN 1901 Hamburg, Germany

DIED 1978 New York, New York

EDUCATION School of Applied Arts, Nuremberg, Germany; School of Applied Arts, Munich, Germany; Academy of Fine Arts, Munich, Germany; Academy of Art, Munich, Germany

SELECTED PUBLIC COLLECTIONS

The Art Institute of Chicago, Chicago, Illinois

The Cleveland Museum of Art, Cleveland, Ohio

Hamburger Kunsthalle, Hamburg, Germany

Musée National d'Art Moderne, Centre Georges Pompidou, Paris, France

Museum Boijmans Van Beuningen, Rotterdam, The Netherlands

The Museum of Modern Art, New York, New York

The RISD Museum, Providence, Rhode Island

Tate Gallery, London, England
Wallraf-Richartz-Museum–Fondation Corboud, Cologne, Germany
Whitney Museum of American Art, New York, New York

JACQUES LIPCHITZ

BORN 1891 Druskieniki, Lithuania

DIED 1973 Capri, Italy

EDUCATION École des Beaux-Arts, Paris, France; Académie Julien, Paris, France

SELECTED PUBLIC COLLECTIONS

Albright-Knox Art Gallery, Buffalo, New York
The Art Institute of Chicago, Chicago, Illinois
The Baltimore Museum of Art, Baltimore, Maryland
The Cleveland Museum of Art, Cleveland, Ohio
The Detroit Institute of Arts, Detroit, Michigan
The Jewish Museum, New York, New York
Los Angeles County Museum of Art, Los Angeles, California
Montreal Museum of Fine Arts, Montreal, Canada
Musée National d'Art Moderne, Centre Georges Pompidou, Paris, France
The Museum of Modern Art, New York, New York
The Phillips Collection, Washington, D.C.
Tate Gallery, London, England
Tel Aviv Museum of Art, Tel Aviv, Israel
Whitney Museum of American Art, New York, New York

MARVIN LIPOFSKY

BORN 1938 Barrington, Illinois

EDUCATION BFA, University of Illinois at Urbana-Champaign, Urbana, Illinois; MS, MFA, University of Wisconsin–Madison, Madison, Wisconsin

Lives and works in Berkeley, California

SELECTED PUBLIC COLLECTIONS

Corning Museum of Glass, Corning, New York
The Detroit Institute of Arts, Detroit, Michigan
Glasmuseet Ebeltoft, Ebeltoft, Denmark
Kunstgewerbemuseum (Museum of Applied Arts), Berlin, Germany
Los Angeles County Museum of Art, Los Angeles, California
The Metropolitan Museum of Art, New York, New York
mudac–Musée de design et d'arts appliqués contemporains, Lausanne, Switzerland
Musée-Atelier du Verre (Glass Museum-Workshop), Sars-Poteries, France
Museum of Arts & Design, New York, New York
The National Museum of Modern Art, Kyoto, Japan
Philadelphia Museum of Art, Philadelphia, Pennsylvania
The Renwick Gallery of the Smithsonian American Art Museum, Smithsonian Institution, Washington, D.C.
Stedelijk Museum, Amsterdam, The Netherlands
Suomen Lasimuseo (Finnish Glass Museum), Riihimäki, Finland
Toledo Museum of Art, Toledo, Ohio

DONALD LIPSKI

BORN 1947 Chicago, Illinois

EDUCATION University of Wisconsin–Madison, Madison, Wisconsin; MFA, Cranbrook Academy of Art, Bloomfield Hills, Michigan

Lives and works in Sag Harbor, New York

SELECTED PUBLIC COLLECTIONS

The Brooklyn Museum of Art, Brooklyn, New York
Corcoran Gallery of Art, Washington, D.C.
Denver Art Museum, Denver, Colorado
The Detroit Institute of Arts, Detroit, Michigan
The Jewish Museum, New York, New York
The Menil Collection, Houston, Texas
The Metropolitan Museum of Art, New York, New York
Miami Art Museum, Miami, Florida
Museum of Contemporary Art, Chicago, Illinois
Museum of Contemporary Art, Miami, Florida
Museum of Contemporary Art, San Diego, California
Museum of Fine Arts, Boston, Massachusetts
The Museum of Fine Arts, Houston, Texas
Walker Art Center, Minneapolis, Minnesota
Whitney Museum of American Art, New York, New York

HARVEY K. LITTLETON

BORN 1922 Corning, New York

EDUCATION BD, University of Michigan, Ann Arbor, Michigan; MFA, Cranbrook Academy of Art, Bloomfield Hills, Michigan

Lives and works in Spruce Pine, North Carolina

SELECTED PUBLIC COLLECTIONS

Corning Museum of Glass, Corning, New York
The Detroit Institute of Arts, Detroit, Michigan
Elvehjem Museum of Art, University of Wisconsin–Madison, Madison, Wisconsin
de Young Museum, San Francisco, California
Glasmuseum, Frauenau, Germany
Hokkaido Museum of Modern Art, Sapporo, Japan
Los Angeles County Museum of Art, Los Angeles, California
The Metropolitan Museum of Art, New York, New York
Museum of Arts & Design, New York, New York
The Museum of Modern Art, New York, New York
The National Museum of Modern Art, Kyoto, Japan
Philadelphia Museum of Art, Philadelphia, Pennsylvania
The Renwick Gallery of the Smithsonian American Art Museum, Smithsonian Institution, Washington, D.C.
Toledo Museum of Art, Toledo, Ohio
Victoria and Albert Museum, London, England

MICHAEL LUCERO

BORN 1953 Tracy, California

EDUCATION BA, Humboldt State University, Arcata, California; MFA, University of Washington, Seattle, Washington

Lives and works in Nyack, New York

SELECTED PUBLIC COLLECTIONS
Arkansas Arts Center, Little Rock, Arkansas
Carnegie Museum of Art, Pittsburgh, Pennsylvania
Everson Museum of Art, Syracuse, New York
Hirshhorn Museum and Sculpture Garden, Smithsonian Institution,
    Washington, D.C.
Los Angeles County Museum of Art, Los Angeles, California
The Metropolitan Museum of Art, New York, New York
The Mint Museum of Craft + Design, Charlotte, North Carolina
Museo Tamayo, Mexico City, Mexico
Museum of Arts & Design, New York, New York
National Gallery of Art, Washington, D.C.
National Museum of Contemporary Art, Seoul, Korea
New Museum of Contemporary Art, New York, New York
San Francisco Museum of Modern Art, San Francisco, California
Seattle Art Museum, Seattle, Washington
Toledo Museum of Art, Toledo, Ohio

MARIA LUGOSSY

BORN 1950 Budapest, Hungary
EDUCATION Hungarian Academy of Applied Arts, Budapest, Hungary
Lives and works in Budapest, Hungary

SELECTED PUBLIC COLLECTIONS
The British Museum, London, England
Corning Museum of Glass, Corning, New York
Glasmuseet Ebeltoft, Ebeltoft, Denmark
Glasmuseum, Frauenau, Germany
Magyar Nemzeti Galéria (Hungarian National Gallery),
    Budapest, Hungary
Musée du Louvre, Paris, France
Musée-Atelier du Verre (Glass Museum-Workshop), Sars-Poteries, France
mudac–Musée de design et d'arts appliqués contemporains,
    Lausanne, Switzerland
Museum of Art, Yokohama, Japan
Museum Kunst Palast, Düsseldorf, Germany
National Liberty Museum, Philadelphia, Pennsylvania
Rijksmuseum, Amsterdam, The Netherlands
Suntory Museum of Art, Tokyo, Japan

FLORA C. MACE

BORN 1949 Exeter, New Hampshire
EDUCATION BS, Fine Arts, Plymouth State College, Plymouth, New
    Hampshire; MFA, University of Illinois, Champaign, Illinois; University
    of Utah, Salt Lake City, Utah
Lives and works in Seattle, Washington

SELECTED PUBLIC COLLECTIONS (collaborative work with Joey Kirkpatrick)
Broadfield House Glass Museum, West Midlands, United Kingdom
Corning Museum of Glass, Corning, New York
The Detroit Institute of Arts, Detroit, Michigan
Glasmuseet Ebeltoft, Ebeltoft, Denmark
Hokkaido Museum of Modern Art, Sapporo, Japan
Kitazawa Glass Museum, Lake Suwa, Japan

Leigh Yawkey Woodson Art Museum, Wausau, Wisconsin
The Metropolitan Museum of Art, New York, New York
mudac–Musée de design et d'arts appliqués contemporains,
    Lausanne, Switzerland
Racine Art Museum, Racine, Wisconsin
The Renwick Gallery of the Smithsonian American Art Museum,
    Smithsonian Institution, Washington, D.C.
Seattle Art Museum, Seattle, Washington
Speed Art Museum, Louisville, Kentucky
Tacoma Art Museum, Tacoma, Washington
Toledo Museum of Art, Toledo, Ohio

JUDY McKIE

BORN 1944 Boston, Massachusetts
EDUCATION BFA, Rhode Island School of Design, Providence,
    Rhode Island
Works in Cambridge, Massachusetts

SELECTED PUBLIC COLLECTIONS
The Albuquerque Museum, Albuquerque, New Mexico
ARC Union, Paris, France
de Young Museum, San Francisco, California
DeCordova Museum and Sculpture Park, Lincoln, Massachusetts
Frederick R. Weisman Art Foundation, Los Angeles, California
Fuller Craft Museum, Brockton, Massachusetts
LongHouse Reserve, East Hampton, New York
Museum of Art, Rhode Island School of Design, Providence,
    Rhode Island
Museum of Arts & Design, New York, New York
Museum of Fine Arts, Boston, Massachusetts
Philadelphia Museum of Art, Philadelphia, Pennsylvania
The Renwick Gallery of the Smithsonian American Art Museum,
    Smithsonian Institution, Washington, D.C.
The Rose Art Museum at Brandeis University, Waltham, Massachusetts
Toledo Museum of Art, Toledo, Ohio
Yale University Art Gallery, New Haven, Connecticut

JOHN McLAUGHLIN

BORN 1898 Sharon, Massachusetts
DIED 1976 Dana Point, California
EDUCATION self-taught

SELECTED PUBLIC COLLECTIONS
Addison Gallery of American Art, Andover, Massachusetts
Albright-Knox Art Gallery, Buffalo, New York
Everson Museum of Art, Syracuse, New York
Inverleith House, Royal Botanic Garden, Edinburgh, Scotland
Joslyn Art Museum, Omaha, Nebraska
The Marion Koogler McNay Art Museum, San Antonio, Texas
Miami Art Museum, Miami, Florida
Oakland Museum of California, Oakland, California
The Renwick Gallery of the Smithsonian American Art Museum,
    Smithsonian Institution, Washington, D.C.
San Diego Museum of Art, San Diego, California

San Francisco Museum of Modern Art, San Francisco, California
Sheldon Memorial Art Gallery, University of Nebraska, Lincoln, Nebraska
Whitney Museum of American Art, New York, New York

MARY MERKEL-HESS

BORN 1949 Gilbertville, Iowa
EDUCATION BA, Marquette University, Milwaukee, Wisconsin; BFA, University of Wisconsin, Milwaukee, Wisconsin; MFA, University of Iowa, Iowa City, Iowa
Lives and works in Iowa City, Iowa

SELECTED PUBLIC COLLECTIONS
The LongHouse Reserve, East Hampton, New York
The Metropolitan Museum of Art, New York, New York
Museum of Arts & Design, New York, New York
Philadelphia Museum of Art, Philadelphia, Pennsylvania
Racine Art Museum, Racine, Wisconsin
University of Iowa Museum of Art, Iowa City, Iowa
The Waterloo Center for the Arts, Waterloo, Iowa

KLAUS MOJE

BORN 1936 Hamburg, Germany
EDUCATION journeyman's certificate, glass cutter and grinder in Moje family workshop, Hamburg, Germany; master's certificate, Rheinbach and Hadamar Glass Schools, Germany
Lives and works in Tanja, New South Wales, Australia

SELECTED PUBLIC COLLECTIONS
Auckland Museum, Auckland, New Zealand
Carnegie Museum of Art, Pittsburgh, Pennsylvania
Corning Museum of Glass, Corning, New York
The Detroit Institute of Arts, Detroit, Michigan
Glasmuseet Ebeltoft, Ebeltoft, Denmark
Hokkaido Museum of Modern Art, Sapporo, Japan
J. & L. Lobmeyr Collection, Vienna, Austria
Kunstgewerbemuseum (Museum of Applied Arts), Berlin, Germany
Los Angeles County Museum of Art, Los Angeles, California
The Metropolitan Museum of Art, New York, New York
mudac–Musée de design et d'arts appliqués contemporains, Lausanne, Switzerland
National Gallery of Victoria, Melbourne, Australia
Royal Scottish Museum, Edinburgh, Great Britain
Toledo Museum of Art, Toledo, Ohio
Victoria and Albert Museum, London, England

WILLIAM MORRIS

BORN 1957 Carmel California
EDUCATION California State University, Chico, California; Central Washington University, Ellensberg, Washington
Works at Pilchuck Glass School in Stanwood, Washington

SELECTED PUBLIC COLLECTIONS
Auckland Museum, Auckland, New Zealand
Carnegie Museum of Art, Pittsburgh, Pennsylvania

Corning Museum of Glass, Corning, New York
Los Angeles County Museum of Art, Los Angeles, California
The Metropolitan Museum of Art, New York, New York
Musée des Arts Décoratifs, Paris, France
Museum of Arts & Design, New York, New York
The Museum of Fine Arts, Houston, Texas
Museum für Kunst und Gewerbe (Museum of Art and Industry), Hamburg, Germany
Norton Museum of Art, West Palm Beach, Florida
The Renwick Gallery of the Smithsonian American Art Museum, Smithsonian Institution, Washington, D.C.
Seattle Art Museum, Seattle, Washington
Toledo Museum of Art, Toledo, Ohio
Victoria and Albert Museum, London, England
Virginia Museum of Fine Arts, Richmond, Virginia

ROBERT MOTHERWELL

BORN 1915 Aberdeen, Washington
DIED 1991 Provincetown, Massachusetts
EDUCATION BA, Stanford University, Stanford, California; California School of Fine Arts, San Francisco, California; Harvard University, Cambridge, Massachusetts; Columbia University, New York, New York

SELECTED PUBLIC COLLECTIONS
Albright-Knox Art Gallery, Buffalo, New York
Art Gallery of Ontario, Toronto, Canada
The Art Institute of Chicago, Chicago, Illinois
The Brooklyn Museum of Art, Brooklyn, New York
The Cleveland Museum of Art, Cleveland, Ohio
Dallas Museum of Art, Dallas, Texas
Hirshhorn Museum and Sculpture Garden, Smithsonian Institution, Washington, D.C.
Los Angeles County Museum of Art, Los Angeles, California
The Metropolitan Museum of Art, New York, New York
The Museum of Modern Art, New York, New York
National Gallery of Art, Washington, D.C.
San Francisco Museum of Modern Art, San Francisco, California
Stedelijk Museum, Amsterdam, The Netherlands
Tel Aviv Museum of Art, Tel Aviv, Israel
Whitney Museum of American Art, New York, New York

JAY MUSLER

BORN 1949 Sacramento, California
EDUCATION California College of Arts and Crafts, San Francisco, California
Lives and works in Berkeley, California

SELECTED PUBLIC COLLECTIONS
Corning Museum of Glass, Corning, New York
The Detroit Institute of Arts, Detroit, Michigan
Hokkaido Museum of Modern Art, Sapporo, Japan
Honolulu Academy of Arts, Honolulu, Hawaii
Kitano Museum, Tokyo, Japan

Los Angeles County Museum of Art, Los Angeles, California

Milwaukee Art Museum, Milwaukee, Wisconsin

mudac–Musée de design et d'arts appliqués contemporains, Lausanne, Switzerland

Museum of American Glass, Wheaton Village, Millville, New Jersey

Oakland Museum of California, Oakland, California

Speed Art Museum, Louisville, Kentucky

Toledo Museum of Art, Toledo, Ohio

Washington University, St. Louis, Missouri

JOEL PHILIP MYERS

BORN 1934 Paterson, New Jersey

EDUCATION Advertising Design, Parsons School of Design, New York, New York; School of Applied Arts, Copenhagan, Denmark; BFA, MFA, Alfred University, Alfred, New York

Lives and works in Marietta, Pennsylvania

SELECTED PUBLIC COLLECTIONS

The Art Institute of Chicago, Chicago, Illinois.

Australian Crafts Council, Sydney, Australia

Corning Museum of Glass, Corning, New York

The Detroit Institute of Arts, Detroit, Michigan

Hokkaido Museum of Modern Art, Sapporo, Japan

Kunstgewerbemuseum (Museum of Applied Arts), Berlin, Germany

Los Angeles County Museum of Art, Los Angeles, California

The Metropolitan Museum of Art, New York, New York

Musée des Arts Décoratifs, Paris, France

Musée du Verre (Glass Museum), Liege, Belgium

Museum Bellerive, Zurich, Switzerland

Museum Boijmans Van Beuningen, Rotterdam, The Netherlands

Museum of Arts & Design, New York, New York

The Renwick Gallery of the Smithsonian American Art Museum, Smithsonian Institution, Washington, D.C.

Röhsska Konstslojdmuseet (Museum of Applied Art and Design), Göteborg, Sweden

MANUEL NERI

BORN 1930 Sanger, California

EDUCATION California College of Arts and Crafts, Oakland, California; California School of Fine Arts, San Francisco, California

Lives and works in Benecia, California

SELECTED PUBLIC COLLECTIONS

Corcoran Gallery of Art, Washington, D.C.

Denver Art Museum, Denver, Colorado

Des Moines Art Center, Des Moines, Iowa

El Paso Museum of Art, El Paso, Texas

Fine Arts Museums of San Francisco, San Francisco, California

Hirshhorn Museum and Sculpture Garden, Smithsonian Institution, Washington, D.C.

Honolulu Academy of Arts, Honolulu, Hawaii

Kemper Museum of Contemporary Art, Kansas City, Missouri

Memphis Brooks Art Museum, Memphis, Tennessee

The Metropolitan Museum of Art, New York, New York

Portland Art Museum, Portland, Oregon

San Diego Museum of Art, San Diego, California

San Francisco Museum of Modern Art, San Francisco, California

Seattle Art Museum, Seattle, Washington

Whitney Museum of American Art, New York, New York

LOUISE NEVELSON

BORN 1900 Kiev, Russia

DIED 1988 New York, New York

EDUCATION Art Students League, New York, New York

SELECTED PUBLIC COLLECTIONS

The Art Institute of Chicago, Chicago, Illinois

Corcoran Gallery of Art, Washington, D.C.

Hirshhorn Museum and Sculpture Garden, Smithsonian Institution, Washington, D.C.

The Metropolitan Museum of Art, New York, New York

Musée d'Art Moderne de la Ville de Paris, Paris, France

The Museum of Modern Art, New York, New York

Solomon R. Guggenheim Museum, New York, New York

Tate Gallery, London, England

Whitney Museum of American Art, New York, New York

TOM PATTI

BORN 1943 Pittsfield, Massachusetts

EDUCATION Boston Museum School, Boston, Massachusetts; Bachelor of Industrial Design, Master of Industrial Design, Pratt Institute School of Art and Design, New York, New York; Perception Theory with Rudolph Arnheim, New School for Social Research, Graduate School of Art and Design, New York, New York

Lives and works in Plainfield, Massachusetts

SELECTED PUBLIC COLLECTIONS

The Art Institute of Chicago, Chicago, Illinois

Carnegie Museum of Art, Pittsburgh, Pennsylvania

Indianapolis Museum of Art, Indianapolis, Indiana

The Metropolitan Museum of Art, New York, New York

The Mint Museum of Craft + Design, Charlotte, North Carolina

Musée des Arts Décoratifs, Paris, France

Museum of Arts & Design, New York, New York

The Museum of Fine Arts, Houston, Texas

Museum of Fine Arts, Boston, Massachusetts

The Museum of Modern Art, New York, New York

Philadelphia Museum of Art, Philadelphia, Pennsylvania

The Saint Louis Art Museum, St. Louis, Missouri

Smithsonian American Art Museum, Smithsonian Institution, Washington, D.C.

Toledo Museum of Art, Toledo, Ohio

Victoria and Albert Museum, London, England

MARK PEISER

BORN 1938 Chicago, Illinois

EDUCATION BS, Institute of Design at the Illinois Institute of Technology, Chicago, Illinois; Purdue University, West Lafayette, Indiana; School of Music, DePaul University, Chicago, Illinois

Lives and works in Penland, North Carolina

SELECTED PUBLIC COLLECTIONS

The Art Institute of Chicago, Chicago, Illinois

Chrysler Museum of Art, Norfolk, Virginia

Cooper-Hewitt, National Design Museum, Smithsonian Institution, New York, New York

Corning Museum of Glass, Corning, New York

La Galerie Internationale du Verre (The International Glass Gallery), Biot, France

Glasmuseet Ebeltoft, Ebeltoft, Denmark

High Museum of Art, Atlanta, Georgia

Hokkaido Museum of Modern Art, Sapporo, Japan

The Mint Museum of Craft + Design, Charlotte, North Carolina

Museum of American Glass, Wheaton Village, Millville, New Jersey

Museum of Art, Lucerne, Switzerland

National Museum of Modern Art, Tokyo, Japan

The People's Republic of China

The Renwick Gallery of the Smithsonian American Art Museum, Smithsonian Institution, Washington, D.C.

RICHARD POUSETTE-DART

BORN 1916 St. Paul, Minnesota

DIED 1992 Suffern, New York

EDUCATION Bard College, Annandale-on-Hudson, New York (left after several months, received honorary degree in 1965)

SELECTED PUBLIC COLLECTIONS

The Brooklyn Museum of Art, Brooklyn, New York

Corcoran Gallery of Art, Washington, D.C.

The Detroit Institute of Arts, Detroit, Michigan

Galleria degli Uffizi, Florence, Italy

Hirshhorn Museum and Sculpture Garden, Smithsonian Institution, Washington, D.C.

Los Angeles County Museum of Art, Los Angeles, California

The Metropolitan Museum of Art, New York, New York

Museum of Fine Arts, Boston, Massachusetts

The Museum of Modern Art, New York, New York

The Newark Museum, Newark, New Jersey

Philadelphia Museum of Art, Philadelphia, Pennsylvania

The Renwick Gallery of the Smithsonian American Art Museum, Smithsonian Institution, Washington, D.C.

Solomon R. Guggenheim Museum, New York, New York

Tel Aviv Museum of Art, Tel Aviv, Israel

Whitney Museum of American Art, New York, New York

DAVID REEKIE

BORN 1947 Hackney (London), England

EDUCATION Stourbridge College of Art, Stourbridge, England; Birmingham College of Art, Birmingham, England

Lives and works in Norwich, England

SELECTED PUBLIC COLLECTIONS

Birmingham Museums & Art Gallery, Birmingham, England

Broadfield House Glass Museum, West Midlands, England

Carnegie Museum of Art, Pittsburgh, Pennsylvania

Glasmuseet Ebeltoft, Ebeltoft, Denmark

Manchester Art Gallery, Manchester, England

Musée-Atelier du Verre (Glass Museum-Workshop), Sars-Poteries, France

National Liberty Museum, Philadelphia, Pennsylvania

Norwich Castle Museum, Norwich, Norfolk, England

Pilkington Glass Museum, St. Helens, England

Portsmouth Museum & Art Gallery, Portsmouth, England

Usher Art Gallery, Lincoln, England

Victoria and Albert Museum, London, England

GERHARD RICHTER

BORN 1932 Dresden, Germany

EDUCATION Art Academy, Dresden, Germany; Academy of Fine Arts, Dresden, Germany; State Academy of the Arts, Düsseldorf, Germany

Lives and works in Cologne, Germany

SELECTED PUBLIC COLLECTIONS

Galerie Neue Meister, Dresden, Germany

Kunstmuseum (Museum of Modern Art), Bonn, Germany

Kunstmuseum Basel, Basel, Switzerland

Louisiana Museum, Humlebaek, Denmark

Musée National d'Art Moderne, Centre Georges Pompidou, Paris, France

Museum Folkwang, Essen, Germany

Museum Kunst Palast, Düsseldorf, Germany

Museum Ludwig, Cologne, Germany

The Museum of Modern Art, New York, New York

Neue Galerie/ Sammlung Ludwig, Aachen, Germany

Neue Nationalgalerie, Berlin, Germany

San Francisco Museum of Modern Art, San Francisco, California

Solomon R. Guggenheim Museum, New York, New York

Städtisches Museum (Municipal Museum), Mönchengladbach, Germany

Van Abbemuseum, Eindhoven, The Netherlands

LARRY RIVERS

BORN 1923 New York, New York

DIED 2002 Southampton, New York

EDUCATION Hans Hofmann School, New York, New York; New York University, New York, New York

SELECTED PUBLIC COLLECTIONS

The Brooklyn Museum of Art, Brooklyn, New York

Georgia Museum of Art, Athens, Georgia

Hirshhorn Museum and Sculpture Garden, Smithsonian Institution, Washington, D.C.

The Metropolitan Museum of Art, New York, New York

The Minneapolis Institute of Arts, Minneapolis, Minnesota
The Museum of Modern Art, New York, New York
National Gallery of Art, Washington, D.C.
The Newark Museum, Newark, New Jersey
Phoenix Art Museum, Phoenix, Arizona
The Renwick Gallery of the Smithsonian American Art Museum,
    Smithsonian Institution, Washington, D.C.
San Diego Museum of Art, San Diego, California
San Francisco Museum of Modern Art, San Francisco, California
Smith College Museum of Art, Northampton, Massachusetts
University of Michigan Museum of Art, Ann Arbor, Michigan
Whitney Museum of American Art, New York, New York

GINNY RUFFNER

BORN 1952 Atlanta, Georgia
EDUCATION BFA, Furman College, Greenville, South Carolina; BFA, MFA,
    University of Georgia, Athens, Georgia
Lives and works in Seattle, Washington
SELECTED PUBLIC COLLECTIONS
Carnegie Museum of Art, Carnegie Institute, Pittsburgh, Pennsylvania
Corning Museum of Glass, Corning, New York
The Detroit Institute of Arts, Detroit, Michigan
Glasmuseum Hentrich, Museum Kunst Palast, Düsseldorf, Germany
Hsinchu Municipal Glass Museum, Hsinchu, Taiwan
Koganezaki Glass Museum, Kamomura, Japan
Los Angeles County Museum of Art, Los Angeles, California
The Metropolitan Museum of Art, New York, New York
The Mint Museum of Craft + Design, Charlotte, North Carolina
mudac–Musée de design et d'arts appliqués contemporains,
    Lausanne, Switzerland
Museum of Arts & Design, New York, New York
Queensland Art Gallery, Brisbane, Australia
The Renwick Gallery of the Smithsonian American Art Museum,
    Smithsonian Institution, Washington, D.C.
Seattle Art Museum, Seattle, Washington
Toledo Museum of Art, Toledo, Ohio

ITALO SCANGA

BORN 1932, Lago (Calabria), Italy
DIED 2001 San Diego, California
EDUCATION BA, MA, Michigan State University, East Lansing, Michigan
SELECTED PUBLIC COLLECTIONS
Albertina Museum, Vienna, Austria
The Art Institute of Chicago, Chicago, Illinois
The Brooklyn Museum of Art, Brooklyn, New York
The Detroit Institute of Arts, Detroit, Michigan
Fogg Art Museum, Harvard University Art Museums,
    Cambridge, Massachusetts
Hirshhorn Museum and Sculpture Garden, Smithsonian Institution,
    Washington, D.C.
Los Angeles County Museum of Art, Los Angeles, California
The Metropolitan Museum of Art, New York, New York

Museum of Contemporary Art, San Diego, California
The Museum of Modern Art, New York, New York
Norton Museum of Art, West Palm Beach, Florida
Philadelphia Museum of Art, Philadelphia, Pennsylvania
RISD Museum, Rhode Island School of Design, Providence,
    Rhode Island
San Diego Museum of Art, San Diego, California
Walker Art Center, Minneapolis, Minnesota

MARY SHAFFER

BORN 1947 Walterboro, South Carolina
EDUCATION BFA, Rhode Island School of Design, Providence, Rhode
    Island; MFA, University of Maryland, College Park, Maryland
Lives and works in Taos, New Mexico, and Marfa, Texas
SELECTED PUBLIC COLLECTIONS
Blumenthal Performing Arts Center, Charlotte, North Carolina
Columbus Museum of Art, Columbus, Ohio
Corning Museum of Glass, Corning, New York
The Detroit Institute of Arts, Detroit, Michigan
Grounds for Sculpture, Hamilton, New Jersey
Indianapolis Museum of Art, Indianapolis, Indiana
The Metropolitan Museum of Art, New York, New York
mudac–Musée de design et d'arts appliqués contemporains,
    Lausanne, Switzerland
Museum Bellerive, Zurich, Switzerland
Museum of Arts & Design, New York, New York
RISD Museum, Rhode Island School of Design, Providence,
    Rhode Island
The National Museum of Modern Art, Kyoto, Japan
The Renwick Gallery of the Smithsonian American Art Museum,
    Smithsonian Institution, Washington, D.C.
Toledo Museum of Art, Toledo, Ohio
U.S. Chancellery, La Paz, Bolivia

CHARLES GREEN SHAW

BORN 1892 New York, New York
DIED 1974 New York, New York
EDUCATION BA, Yale University, New Haven, Connecticut; Art Students
    League, New York, New York
SELECTED PUBLIC COLLECTIONS
Addison Gallery of American Art, Andover, Massachusetts
The Baltimore Museum of Art, Baltimore, Maryland
The Brooklyn Museum of Art, Brooklyn, New York
Carnegie Museum of Art, Pittsburgh, Pennsylvania
High Museum of Art, Atlanta, Georgia
Museum of Fine Arts, Boston, Massachusetts
The Newark Museum, Newark, New Jersey
Pennsylvania Academy of the Fine Arts, Philadelphia, Pennsylvania
The Phillips Collection, Washington, D.C.
Phoenix Art Museum, Phoenix, Arizona
The Renwick Gallery of the Smithsonian American Art Museum,
    Smithsonian Institution, Washington, D.C.

San Francisco Museum of Modern Art, San Francisco, California
Solomon R. Guggenheim Museum, New York, New York
Whitney Museum of American Art, New York, New York
Yale University Art Gallery, New Haven, Connecticut

JESÚS RAFAEL SOTO

BORN 1923 Ciudad Bolívar, Venezuela
DIED 2005 Paris, France
EDUCATION Academy of Fine Arts, Caracas, Venezuela
SELECTED PUBLIC COLLECTIONS
Albright-Knox Art Gallery, Buffalo, New York
Cali Institute of Fine Arts, Cali, Colombia
Galleria Nazionale d'Arte Moderna, Rome, Italy
Hara Museum of Contemporary Art, Tokyo, Japan
Moderna Museet, Stockholm, Sweden
Musée d'Art Contemporain de Montreal, Montreal, Canada
Musée National d'Art Moderne, Centre Georges Pompidou,
    Paris, France
Museo Nacional Centro de Arte Reina Sofía, Madrid, Spain
Museo Nacional de Bellas Artes, Buenos Aires, Argentina
Museo Tamayo, Mexico City, Mexico
National Gallery of Victoria, Melbourne, Australia
Stedelijk Museum, Amsterdam, The Netherlands
University City, Caracas, Venezuela
Tate Gallery, London, England
Tel Aviv Museum of Art, Tel Aviv, Israel

PAUL JOSEPH STANKARD

BORN 1943 Attleboro, Massachusetts
EDUCATION Salem Technical Institute, Carneys Point, New Jersey
Lives and works in Mantua, New Jersey
SELECTED PUBLIC COLLECTIONS
The Art Institute of Chicago, Chicago, Illinois
The Brooklyn Museum, Brooklyn, New York
Corning Museum of Glass, Corning, New York
Glasmuseet Ebeltoft, Ebeltoft, Denmark
Hsinchu Municipal Glass Museeum, Hsinchu, Taiwan
Hokkaido Museum of Modern Art, Sapporo, Japan
The Metropolitan Museum of Art, New York, New York
Musée des Arts Décoratifs, Paris, France
Museum of American Glass, Wheaton Village, Millville, New Jersey
Museum of Arts & Design, New York, New York
Museum of Fine Arts, Boston, Massachusetts
Philadelphia Museum of Art, Philadelphia, Pennsylvania
The Renwick Gallery of the Smithsonian American Art Museum,
    Smithsonian Institution, Washington, D.C.
Toledo Museum of Art, Toledo, Ohio
Victoria and Albert Museum, London, England

THERMAN STATOM

BORN 1953 Winterhaven, Florida
EDUCATION Pilchuck Glass School, Stanwood, Washington; BFA,
    Rhode Island School of Design, Providence, Rhode Island; MFA,
    Pratt Institute, Brooklyn, New York
Lives and works in Los Angeles, California
SELECTED PUBLIC COLLECTIONS
Bergstrom-Mahler Museum, Neenah, Wisconsin
California African American Museum, Los Angeles, California
Corning Museum of Glass, Corning, New York
The Detroit Institute of Arts, Detroit, Michigan
Henry Art Gallery, University of Washington, Seattle, Washington
High Museum of Art, Atlanta, Georgia
Oakland Museum of California, Oakland, California
Portable Works Collection, City of Seattle, Seattle, Washington
Toledo Museum of Art, Toledo, Ohio

FRANK STELLA

BORN 1936 Malden, Massachusetts
EDUCATION AB, Princeton University, Princeton, New Jersey
Lives and works in New York, New York
SELECTED PUBLIC COLLECTIONS
Albright-Knox Art Gallery, Buffalo, New York
The Art Institute of Chicago, Chicago, Illinois
Kaiser Wilhelm Museum, Krefeld, Germany
Musée National d'Art Moderne, Centre Georges Pompidou,
    Paris, France
The Museum of Modern Art, New York, New York
San Francisco Museum of Modern Art, San Francisco, California
Stedelijk Museum, Amsterdam, The Netherlands
Van Abbemuseum, Eindhoven, The Netherlands
Walker Art Center, Minneapolis, Minnesota
Whitney Museum of American Art, New York, New York

SUSAN STINSMUEHLEN-AMEND

BORN 1948 Baltimore, Maryland
EDUCATION Hood College, Frederick, Maryland; University of Texas,
    Austin, Texas
Lives and works in Ojai, California
SELECTED PUBLIC COLLECTIONS
Corning Museum of Glass, Corning, New York
The Detroit Institute of Arts, Detroit, Michigan
The Jewish Museum, New York, New York
Leigh Yawkey Woodson Art Museum, Wausau, Wisconsin
Los Angeles County Museum of Art, Los Angeles, California
Museum of Arts & Design, New York, New York
Nishida Museum, Toyoma, Japan
Oakland Museum of California, Oakland, California
Pilchuck Glass School, Stanwood, Washington
The Renwick Gallery of the Smithsonian American Art Museum,
    Smithsonian Institution, Washington, D.C.
Wagga Wagga Art Gallery, Wagga Wagga, New South Wales, Australia

LINO TAGLIAPIETRA

BORN 1934, Murano (Venice), Italy

EDUCATION apprenticeship with Archimede Seguso

Lives and works in Seattle, Washington, and Murano, Italy

SELECTED PUBLIC COLLECTIONS

Corning Museum of Glass, Corning, New York

Danish Royal Museum, Copenhagen, Denmark

The Detroit Institute of Arts, Detroit, Michigan

Glasmuseet Ebeltoft, Ebeltoft, Denmark

de Young Museum, San Francisco, California

Kestner Museum, Hanover, Germany

mudac–Musée de design et d'arts appliqués contemporains,
    Lausanne, Switzerland

Musée des Arts Décoratifs, Paris, France

Museo del Vidrio (Glass Museum), Monterrey, Mexico

Museum Boijmans Van Beuningen, Rotterdam, The Netherlands

The Museum of Glass, Tacoma, Washington

National Museum of Modern Art, Tokyo, Japan

Palazzo Grassi, Venice, Italy

Seattle Art Museum, Seattle, Washington

Victoria and Albert Museum, London, England

AKIO TAKAMORI

BORN 1950 Nobeoka, Japan

EDUCATION BFA, Kansas City Art Institute, Kansas City, Missouri;
    MFA, Alfred University, Alfred, New York

Lives and works in Seattle, Washington

SELECTED PUBLIC COLLECTIONS

Archie Bray Foundation for the Ceramic Arts, Helena, Montana

Arizona State University Art Museum, Tempe, Arizona

Arkansas Arts Center, Little Rock, Arkansas

Carnegie Museum of Art, Pittsburgh, Pennsylvania

Kansas City Art Institute, Kansas City, Missouri

The Kinsey Institute, Bloomington, Indiana

Los Angeles County Museum of Art, Los Angeles, California

Museum Het Kruithuis, 's-Hertogenbosch, The Netherlands

Museum of Arts & Design, New York, New York

Museum of Contemporary Ceramic Art, Shigaraki, Japan

National Museum of History, Taipei, Taiwan

The Schein-Joseph International Museum of Ceramic Art, Alfred, New York

Spencer Museum of Art: University of Kansas, Lawrence, Kansas

Taipei Fine Arts Museum, Taipei, Taiwan

Victoria and Albert Museum, London, England

CAPPY THOMPSON

BORN 1952 Alexandria, Virginia

EDUCATION Fairhaven College, Bellingham, Washington; The Factory
    of Visual Arts, Seattle, Washington; BA, Evergreen State College,
    Olympia, Washington

Lives and works in Seattle, Washington

SELECTED PUBLIC COLLECTIONS

The Art Gallery of Western Australia, Perth, Australia

Birmingham Museums & Art Gallery, Birmingham, United Kingdom

Chrysler Museum of Art, Norfolk, Virginia

Corning Museum of Glass, Corning, New York

Hokkaido Museum of Modern Art, Sapporo, Japan

Huntsville Museum of Art, Huntsville, Alabama

Montgomery Museum of Fine Arts, Montgomery, Alabama

Museum of Arts & Design, New York, New York

The Museum of Glass, Tacoma, Washington

Seattle-Tacoma International Airport, Seattle, Washington

Tacoma Art Museum, Tacoma, Washington

Toyama City Institute of Glass Art, Toyama, Japan

STEVE TOBIN

BORN 1957 Philadelphia, Pennsylvania

EDUCATION BS, Tulane University, New Orleans, Louisiana

Lives and works near Philadelphia, Pennsylvania

SELECTED PUBLIC COLLECTIONS

American Center, Helsinki, Finland

Boca Raton Museum of Art, Boca Raton, Florida

Lowe Art Museum, University of Miami, Coral Gables, Florida

mudac–Musée de design et d'arts appliqués contemporains,
    Lausanne, Switzerland

Museum of American Glass, Wheaton Village, Millville, New Jersey

Museum of Arts & Design, New York, New York

New Orleans Museum of Art, New Orleans, Louisiana

Philadelphia Museum of Art, Philadelphia, Pennsylvania

Philip and Muriel Berman Museum of Art at Ursinus College,
    Collegeville, Pennsylvania

Retretti Art Center, Punkaharju, Finland

The State Museum of Pennsylvania, Harrisburg, Pennsylvania

The White House, Washington, D.C.

JOAQUÍN TORRES-GARCÍA

BORN 1874 Montevideo, Uruguay

DIED 1949 Montevideo, Uruguay

EDUCATION Official School of Fine Arts, Barcelona, Spain; Academia
    Baixas, Barcelona, Spain

SELECTED PUBLIC COLLECTIONS

Albright-Knox Art Gallery, Buffalo, New York

Art Museum of the Americas, Washington, D.C.

The Baltimore Museum of Art, Baltimore, Maryland

Hirshhorn Museum and Sculpture Garden: Smithsonian Institution,
    Washington, D.C.

The Jack S. Blanton Museum of Art, University of Texas at Austin,
    Austin, Texas

Musée d'Art Moderne de la Ville de Paris, Paris, France

Museo de Arte Contemporaneo de Caracas Sofía Imber, Caracas,
    Venezuela

Museo Nacional Centro de Arte Reina Sofía, Madrid, Spain

Museo Nacional de Artes Plásticas (National Museum of the
    Plastic Arts), Parque Rodó, Montevideo, Uruguay

Museo Nacional de Bellas Artes, Buenos Aires, Argentina

Museo Torres García, Montevideo, Uruguay
The Museum of Modern Art, New York, New York
Philadelphia Museum of Art, Philadelphia, Pennsylvania
San Francisco Museum of Modern Art, San Francisco, California
Solomon R. Guggenheim Museum, New York, New York

KARLA TRINKLEY

BORN 1956 Yardley, Pennsylvania
EDUCATION BFA, Tyler School of Art, Elkins Park, Pennsylvania;
    Rhode Island School of Design, Providence, Rhode Island
Lives and works in Barto, Pennsylvania
SELECTED PUBLIC COLLECTIONS
Akron Art Museum, Akron, Ohio
Corning Museum of Glass, Corning, New York
de Young Museum, San Francisco, California
Hokkaido Museum of Modern Art, Sapporo, Japan
Huntington Galleries, Park Hills, West Virginia
Indianapolis Museum of Art, Indianapolis, Indiana
Los Angeles County Museum of Art, Los Angeles, California
National Gallery of Victoria, Melbourne, Australia
National Liberty Museum, Philadelphia, Pennsylvania
Philadelphia Museum of Art, Philadelphia, Pennsylvania
Shimonoseki City Art Museum, Shimonoseki, Japan
The Renwick Gallery of the Smithsonian American Art Museum,
    Smithsonian Institution, Washington, D.C.
Toledo Museum of Art, Toledo, Ohio

BERTIL VALLIEN

BORN 1938 Stockholm, Sweden
EDUCATION Konstfack School of Arts, Crafts and Design in Stockholm,
    Sweden; School for Advanced Industrial Design, Stockholm, Sweden
Lives and works in Eriksmala, Sweden
SELECTED PUBLIC COLLECTIONS
The Art Gallery of Western Australia, Perth, Australia
The Art Institute of Chicago, Chicago, Illinois
Corning Museum of Glass, Corning, New York
The Detroit Institute of Arts, Detroit, Michigan
Die Neue Sammlung, State Museum of Applied Art, Munich, Germany
Everson Museum of Art, Syracuse, New York
Glasmuseet Ebeltoft, Ebeltoft, Denmark
mudac–Musée de design et d'arts appliqués contemporains,
    Lausanne, Switzerland
Museum of Art, Yokohama, Japan
National Museum of Modern Art, Tokyo, Japan
The National Museum of Modern Art, Kyoto, Japan
Nationalmuseum, Stockholm, Sweden
Röhsska Konstslojdmuseet (Museum of Applied Art and Design),
    Goteborg, Sweden
The State Hermitage Museum, St. Petersburg, Russia
Toledo Museum of Art, Toledo, Ohio
Victoria and Albert Museum, London, England

MARY VAN CLINE

BORN 1954 Dallas, Texas
EDUCATION BFA, North Texas State University, Denton, Texas; MA,
    Texas Women's University, Denton, Texas; Penland School of Crafts,
    Penland, North Carolina; MFA, Massachusetts College of Art, Boston,
    Massachusetts
Lives and works in Seattle, Washington
SELECTED PUBLIC COLLECTIONS
Corning Museum of Glass, Corning, New York
The Detroit Institute of Arts, Detroit, Michigan
La Galerie Internationale du Verre (The International Glass Gallery),
    Biot, France
Glasmuseet Ebeltoft, Ebeltoft, Denmark
Hokkaido Museum of Modern Art, Sapporo, Japan
Huntington Museum of Art, Huntington, West Virginia
Hunter Museum of American Art, Chattanooga, Tennessee
Huntsville Museum of Art, Huntsville, Alabama
Kanazawa International Design Institute, Kanazawa, Japan
Museum für Kunst und Gewerbe (Museum of Art and Industry),
    Hamburg, Germany
Museum of American Glass, Wheaton Village, Millville, New Jersey
Niijima Contemporary Glass Art Museum, Niijima, Japan
Philadelphia Museum of Art, Philadelphia, Pennsylvania
Racine Art Museum, Racine, Wisconsin
The Renwick Gallery of the Smithsonian American Art Museum,
    Smithsonian Institution, Washington, D.C.

JANUSZ WALENTYNOWICZ

BORN 1956, Dygowo, Poland
EDUCATION School of Decorative Art, Copenhagen, Denmark; Illinois
    State University, Normal, Illinois
Lives and works in Clinton, Illinois
SELECTED PUBLIC COLLECTIONS
Arkansas Arts Center, Little Rock, Arkansas
Chrysler Museum of Art, Norfolk, Virginia
The Cleveland Art Museum, Cleveland, Ohio
The Collection of the Regional Council of Upper Normandy,
    Rouen, France
Columbus Museum of Art, Columbus, Ohio
Corning Museum of Glass, Corning, New York
de Young Museum, California
The Detroit Institute of Arts, Detroit, Michigan
Glasmuseet Ebeltoft, Ebeltoft, Denmark.
Her Majesty the Queen's Collection, Copenhagen, Denmark
Hsinchu Municipal Glass Museeum, Hsinchu, Taiwan
Museum Beelden aan Zee, Scheveningen, The Netherlands
Museum of Arts & Design, New York, New York
National Liberty Museum, Philadelphia, Pennsylvania
Rockford Art Museum, Rockford, Illinois

PATTI WARASHINA

BORN 1940 Spokane, Washington

EDUCATION BA, MFA, University of Washington, Seattle, Washington

Lives and works in Seattle, Washington

SELECTED PUBLIC COLLECTIONS

Arkansas Arts Center, Little Rock, Arkansas

The Art Gallery of Western Australia, Perth, Australia

The Detroit Institute of Arts, Detroit, Michigan

Everson Museum of Art, Syracuse, New York

Frederick R. Weisman Museum, University of Minnesota,
    Minneapolis, Minnesota

Los Angeles County Museum of Art, Los Angeles, California

The Mint Museum of Craft + Design, Charlotte, North Carolina

Museum of Arts & Design, New York City, New York

The National Museum of Modern Art, Kyoto, Japan

The Renwick Gallery of the Smithsonian American Art Museum,
    Smithsonian Institution, Washington, D.C.

Seattle Art Museum, Seattle, Washington

Tacoma Art Museum, Tacoma, Washington

World Ceramic Exposition Korea (WOCEK) Collection, Icheon World
    Ceramic Center, Icheon, Korea

JAMES WATKINS

BORN 1955 New Iberia, Louisiana

EDUCATION BA, Eisenhower College, Seneca Falls, New York; MFA,
    Rhode Island School of Design, Providence, Rhode Island

Lives and works in Pawtucket, Rhode Island

SELECTED PUBLIC COLLECTIONS

Château Pichon-Longueville, Paulliac, France

Corning Museum of Glass, Corning, New York

Ernsting Stiftung Glass Museum, Coesfeld, Germany

Glasmuseum, Frauenau, Germany

Huntington Museum of Art, Huntington, West Virginia

Leigh Yawkey Woodson Art Museum, Wausau, Wisconsin

The Mint Museum of Craft + Design, Charlotte, North Carolina

mudac–Musée de design et d'arts appliqués contemporains,
    Lausanne, Switzerland

Musée-Atelier du Verre (Glass Museum-Workshop), Sars-Poteries,
    France

Museum of Art, Rhode Island School of Design, Providence,
    Rhode Island

Museum of Arts & Design, New York, New York

Pilchuck Glass School, Stanwood, Washington

Racine Art Museum, Racine, Wisconsin

The Renwick Gallery of the Smithsonian American Art Museum:
    Smithsonian Institution, Washington, D.C.

Speed Art Museum, Louisville, Kentucky

STEVEN I. WEINBERG

BORN 1954 Brooklyn, New York

EDUCATION BFA, New York State College of Ceramics, Alfred University,
    Alfred, New York; MFA, Rhode Island School of Design, Providence,
    Rhode Island

Works in Pawtucket, Rhode Island

SELECTED PUBLIC COLLECTIONS

Chrysler Museum of Art, Norfolk, Virginia

Corning Museum of Art, Corning, New York

High Museum of Art, Atlanta, Georgia

Hokkaido Museum of Modern Art, Sapporo, Japan

Los Angeles County Museum of Art, Los Angeles, California

The Metropolitan Museum of Art, New York, New York

Milwaukee Art Museum, Milwaukee, Wisconsin

mudac–Musée de design et d'arts appliqués contemporains,
    Lausanne, Switzerland

Musée des Arts Décoratifs, Paris, France

Museum Kunst Palast, Düsseldorf, Germany

Museum of Arts & Design, New York, New York

The National Museum of Modern Art, Kyoto, Japan

The Renwick Gallery of the Smithsonian American Art Museum,
    Smithsonian Institution, Washington, D.C.

Toledo Museum of Art, Toledo, Ohio

Victoria and Albert Museum, London, England

TOM WESSELMANN

BORN 1931 Cincinnati, Ohio

EDUCATION Art Academy of Cincinnati, Cincinnati, Ohio; Hiram College,
    Hiram, Ohio; BA, University of Cincinnati, Cincinnati, Ohio; Cooper
    Union School of Art, New York, New York

Lives and works in New York, New York

SELECTED PUBLIC COLLECTIONS

Albright-Knox Art Gallery, Buffalo, New York

Cincinnati Art Museum, Cincinnati, Ohio

Dallas Museum of Art, Dallas, Texas

The Minneapolis Institute of Arts, Minneapolis, Minnesota

The Museum of Modern Art, New York, New York

Philadelphia Museum of Art, Philadelphia, Pennsylvania

Walker Art Center, Minneapolis, Minnesota

Wallraf-Richartz-Museum–Fondation Corboud, Cologne, Germany

Whitney Museum of American Art, New York, New York

Worcester Art Museum, Worcester, Massachusetts

JOHN WILDE

BORN 1919 Milwaukee, Wisconsin

EDUCATION BS, MS, University of Wisconsin–Madison, Madison,
    Wisconsin

Lives and works in Evansville, Wisconsin

SELECTED PUBLIC COLLECTIONS

The Art Institute of Chicago, Chicago, Illinois

Carnegie Museum of Art, Carnegie Institute, Pittsburgh, Pennsylvania

The DeBeers Museum, Johannesburg, South Africa

The Detroit Institute of Arts, Detroit, Michigan
Elvehjem Museum of Art, University of Wisconsin–Madison,
    Madison, Wisconsin
Milwaukee Art Museum, Milwaukee, Wisconsin
Museum of Contemporary Art, Chicago, Illinois
The Museum of Modem Art, New York, New York
National Academy Museum, New York, New York
Pennsylvania Academy of Fine Arts, Philadelphia, Pennsylvania
Smithsonian American Art Museum, Smithsonian Institution,
    Washington, D.C.
Wadsworth Atheneum Museum of Art, Hartford, Connecticut
Walker Art Center, Minneapolis, Minnesota
Whitney Museum of American Art, New York, New York
Yale University Art Gallery, New Haven, Connecticut

ANN WOLFF

BORN 1937 Lübeck, Germany
EDUCATION Academy of Design, Ulm, Germany
Lives and works in Kosta, Sweden, and Berlin, Germany
SELECTED PUBLIC COLLECTIONS
Corning Museum of Glass, Corning, New York
Glasmuseet Ebeltoft, Ebeltoft, Denmark
Hokkaido Museum of Modern Art, Sapporo, Japan
J. & L. Lobmeyr Collection, Vienna, Austria
Kunstsammlungen der Veste Coburg (Coburg Museum),
    Coburg, Germany
Leigh Yawkey Woodson Art Museum, Wausau, Wisconsin
The Metropolitan Museum of Art, New York, New York
Musée-Atelier du Verre (Glass Museum-Workshop),
    Sars-Poteries, France
Museum Bellerive, Zurich, Switzerland
Museum für Kunst und Gewerbe (Museum of Art and Industry),
    Hamburg, Germany
National Museum of Modern Art, Tokyo, Japan
Nationalmuseum, Stockholm, Sweden
Stedelijk Museum, Amsterdam, The Netherlands
Toledo Museum of Art, Toledo, Ohio
Victoria and Albert Museum, London, England

JACK YOUNGERMAN

BORN 1926 Louisville, Kentucky
EDUCATION University of North Carolina, Chapel Hill, North Carolina;
    BA, University of Missouri, Columbia, Missouri; École des Beaux-Arts,
    Paris, France
Lives and works in Bridgehampton, New York
SELECTED PUBLIC COLLECTIONS
The Art Institute of Chicago, Chicago, Illinois
The Baltimore Museum of Art, Baltimore, Maryland
Carnegie Museum of Art, Pittsburgh, Pennsylvania
Corcoran Gallery of Art, Washington, D.C.
Hirshhorn Museum and Sculpture Garden, Smithsonian Institution,
    Washington, D.C.

Musée de Grenoble, Grenoble, France
The Museum of Fine Arts, Houston, Texas
The Museum of Modern Art, New York, New York
The Newark Museum, Newark, New Jersey
The Phillips Collection, Washington, D.C.
The Renwick Gallery of the Smithsonian American Art Museum,
    Smithsonian Institution, Washington, D.C.
Solomon R. Guggenheim Museum, New York, New York
Walker Art Center, Minneapolis, Minnesota
Whitney Museum of American Art, New York, New York
Yale University Art Gallery, New Haven, Connecticut

CZESLAW ZUBER

BORN 1948 Przybylowice, Poland
EDUCATION School of Fine Arts, Wroclaw, Poland
Lives and works in Paris, France
SELECTED PUBLIC COLLECTIONS
Corning Museum of Glass, Corning, New York
The Detroit Institute of Arts, Detroit, Michigan
Glasmuseum, Frauenau, Germany
Glasmuseum Hentrich, Museum Kunst Palast, Düsseldorf, Germany
Museum für Kunst und Gewerbe (Museum of Art and Industry),
    Hamburg, Germany
Muzeum Okregowe, Jelenia Gora, Poland
mudac–Musée de design et d'arts appliqués contemporains,
    Lausanne, Switzerland
Musée des Arts Décoratifs, Paris, France
Musée-Atelier du Verre (Glass Museum-Workshop), Sars-Poteries,
    France
Museo Nacional de Ceramica "Gonzalez Marti," Valencia, Spain
Museum Bellerive, Zurich, Switzerland
Muzeum Narodowe (National Museum), Wroclaw, Poland
National Liberty Museum, Philadelphia, Pennsylvania
National Museum of Modern Art, Tokyo, Japan
Nordenfjeldske Kunstindustrimuseum (National Decorative Arts
    Museum), Trondheim, Norway

DUAL VISION: THE CHAZEN COLLECTION

SILAS KOPF
Remembering Louis (desk),
1993
walnut, maple, ebony,
marquetry
27 x 62 ⅝ x 24 ½

Page numbers for color plates are in bold.

A

Adams, Hank Murta 46, **121,** 176
Archipenko, Alexander 13, **143,** 176
Arneson, Robert 6, 44, **169,** 176-7
Autio, Rudy 23, **154,** 177
Avery, Milton 13, 38, **86,** 177

B

Bauermeister, Mary **170-1,** 177
Beck, Rick **168,** 177
Ben Tré, Howard 13, 53, **116, 117,** 177-8
Bolotowsky, Ilya 31, **118,** 178
Brychtová, Jaroslava 11, 21, 47-8, 53, 55, **107, 166,** 178
Bubacco, Lucio **114,** 178

C

Calder, Alexander 32, 34-5, **76-7,** 178
Carlson, William 54, **138,** 179
Caro, Sir Anthony 22, **104,** 179
Cash, Sidney **66,** 179
Chia, Sandro 35, 37, **81,** 179
Chihuly, Dale 6, 10, 11, 13, 24, 56, **140, 159,** 179-80
Clayman, Daniel 24, 25, **134,** 180

D

Dailey, Dan 21, 47, **64, 137,** 180
de Amaral, Olga **113,** 180
Diller, Burgoyne 14, 31, 33 (fn. 6), **123,** 180-1
Dine, Jim 7, 24, **152,** 181
Dubuffet, Jean 13, 30, 35-6, 39, **84-5, 105,** 181

E

Eisch, Erwin 7, 45, **74-5,** 181

F

Frey, Viola 22, 23, **146, 147,** 181
Fujita, Kyoku **115,** 182

G

Garman, Ed 31, **93,** 182
Glancy, Michael 25, **161,** 182
Grosz, George **73,** 182

H

Held, Al 34, **120,** 182
Hockney, David 10, 30, 36, **132,** 183
Hofmann, Hans 30, 33, 35, **97,** 183

I

Isupov, Sergei 7, 14, 23, **149,** 183

K

Kirkpatrick, Joey 21, **94,** 183
Kopf, Silas 183-4, **196-7**
Kuhn, Jon 53-4, **122,** 184

L

Labino, Dominick 6, 56, **158,** 184
Libenský, Stanislav 6, 7, 11, 21, 47-8, 53, 55, **107, 166,** 184
Lichtenstein, Roy 10, 14, 31-2, 36, 38, **108-9, 150-1,** 184
Lindner, Richard 7, 30, 37, **164,** 184-5
Lipchitz, Jacques 13, 43-4, **62,** 185
Lipofsky, Marvin 24, 56, **153,** 185
Lipski, Donald 21, **63,** 185
Littleton, Harvey K. 6, 10, 11, 55, **136, 160,** 185
Lucero, Michael **133,** 186-7
Lugossy, Maria 25, 53, **99,** 186

M

Mace, Flora C. 21, **94,** 186
McKie, Judy 21, **156,** 186
McLaughlin, John 31, **95,** 186-7
Merkel-Hess, Mary **128,** 187
Moje, Klaus 56, **155,** 187
Morris, William 6, 13, 14, 26, **72, 80, 119,** 187
Motherwell, Robert 7, 13, 34, **126-7,** 187
Musler, Jay **172,** 188
Myers, Joel Philip 56, **89,** 188

N

Neri, Manuel 23-4, **67,** 188
Nevelson, Louise 32-3, **106,** 188

P

Patti, Tom 21, 53, **98,** 188
Peiser, Mark 11, 55, **92,** 189
Pousette-Dart, Richard 13, 14, 33-4, 35, 39, **68, 112, 135,** 189

R

Reekie, David **101,** 189
Richter, Gerhard 13, 30, 35, **61,** 189
Rivers, Larry 7, 10, 37, 38, **71,** 189-90
Ruffner, Ginny 13, 25-6, **88,** 190

S

Scanga, Italo **142,** 190
Shaffer, Mary 6, 13, 25, 54, **110, 141,** 190
Shaw, Charles Green 31, 35, **167,** 190-1
Soto, Jesús Rafael 30, 31, 32, 39, **100,** 191
Stankard, Paul **111,** 191
Statom, Therman **124,** 191
Stella, Frank 13, 35, **102-3,** 191
Stinsmuehlen-Amend, Susan 54-5, **162-3,** 191-2

T

Tagliapietra, Lino 6, 21, 55, **69,** 192
Takamori, Akio 44-5, **139,** 192
Thompson, Cappy **87,** 192
Tobin, Steve **129,** 192
Torres-García, Joaquín 30, 32, **65,** 192-3
Trinkley, Karla **83,** 193

V

Vallien, Bertil 12, 26, 45-6, **144, 145,** 193
Van Cline, Mary **125,** 193

W

Walentynowicz, Janusz 21, 46, **130, 165,** 193
Warashina, Patti 45, **157,** 194
Watkins, James **70,** 194
Weinberg, Steven I. 21, 52, **78, 79,** 194
Wesselmann, Tom 37, **90-1,** 194
Wilde, John 13, 23, 30, 38, **148,** 194-5
Wolff, Ann 23, **131,** 195

Y

Youngerman, Jack **82,** 195

Z

Zuber, Czeslaw 47, **96,** 195